When Grandpa Was a Kid

*Rich,
We were all kids once. Enjoy!
Paul*

When Grandpa Was a Kid
Growing up in the Pacific Northwest

Paul Strand

Amber Leaf Publishing
Seattle

When Grandpa Was a Kid
Copyright © 2011 by Paul Strand

ISBN-13: 978-1466263437
ISBN-10: 1466263431
Library of Congress Catalog Number: 2011917689

Amber Leaf Publishing
4308 29th Ave. SE
Lacey, WA 98503

Printed in the United States of America

To grandpas everywhere

To my wife Karen who spent hours editing
and encouraging me with her kind words.

Prologue

I never knew my paternal grandfather, or even his middle name. Of his father, I know nothing at all. My mother's ancestors are hidden in the mysteries of a Swedish adoption. This book will allow my own descendents to know something of their roots, as I share a piece of history viewed through the eyes of a child.

All the events recalled here are as they happened. Because I moved so much, a few events may be out of order, but all are accurate. Some of the quotes are verbatim, others approximate what I remember.

As I thought out the days of my childhood I was delighted that old memories came to surface and names were remembered. Even long ago aromas filled my nostrils.

Chapter 1

Moses Lake

Peeling potatoes at 4 o'clock in the morning to the hum of a refrigerator compressor was hypnotic. The kitchen of Nona's Café was hot, even with the back door propped open to the summer night. I sat on an upside-down, empty five-gallon shortening can, fighting sleep, placing peeled potatoes into a French fry cutter. With the pull of a handle the fries fell into another five-gallon shortening can filled with cold water and a chemical called Potato White, which kept the spuds from turning brown. The formaldehyde in it also kept the salads looking fresh.

I had to have all the potatoes ready before the construction workers and farmers showed up for breakfast. The hash browns were steamed, grated and heaped on plates in the fridge ready for the cook to reach in for a handful to slap into a puddle of oil on the hot grill.

Before long, the French fries were ready. I dragged the potato sack to its place in the back of the kitchen. I could feel the cool morning air drift in through the open door. It brought with it the scent of fresh desert air and the color of sunrise. But there was no time to rest. Soon the jukebox kicked in filling the café with popular music, and the waitresses shouted orders into the kitchen, "ham an' over easy", "short stack," while "order up" came back from the cook.

Sleep was forgotten as the kitchen went into action

and dirty dishes started flooding my sinks.

Every morning, at our busiest time, a cop and a trustee from the Moses Lake jail came in. They sat at the counter and drank free coffee while they waited for a large wooden box of pancakes and a big pot of coffee they would bring back to the prisoners. The trustee had to carry both containers. All the cop had to do was stick a thumb in his belt and look as tough as a short fat cop could.

My all night shift ended at 8 a.m. I pulled off my wet apron and took a seat in a back booth. Union dishwashers got two free meals per shift. In between times I was allowed to drink unlimited amounts of pop and coffee. A piece of pie occasionally disappeared when there was time. By the time I sat down, the café was only half full.

"What'll ya have, Paul?" one of the pretty young waitresses asked me. They were all young and pretty, but not as young as me. I was only sixteen.

"How about sausage and eggs over medium?" That's what I ate every morning. The sausages were huge, with two eggs, a pile of my hash browns, and toast with jam on an oval platter. "Can I have a large milk too, please?"

"Of course you can."

Everyone treated me kindly and even watched their language around me, probably because my stepfather, Bill, was the manager. I lit a cigarette and contemplated my walk home. We lived about three miles from the café. Four of us, including my mom and Bill's eight-year-old son, Duane, lived crammed together in a hot little one bedroom trailer house that baked in the August sun.

I stuck my fork into a sausage, causing the platter to wobble and rattle on the table. I tried to be more careful, not wanting to draw attention to myself, but it rattled some more. I looked up and the waitress was grinning at me.

"Looks like you got the warped platter, Paul."

"As usual," I said, as I stuck a napkin under its corner.

I finished my breakfast and sleepily stared through the café listening, for the umpteenth time, to a popular country song called, "These Hands." The words haunted me, "Lord above hear my plea, when it's time to judge me, take a look at these hard working hands." I looked at my young, smooth dishwater hands with a freshly healed cut from a broken glass in the dish water. I thought of myself as a hard-working man who had just finished a night's labor. *Would I someday be an old man trying to get into heaven on the weight of my hard working hands?*

Paul age 16 wearing a leopard shirt bought from his own wages

The waitress came back, sat across from me and chatted for a while. When she got up she asked, "you want anything else?"

Since I wasn't old enough to buy cigarettes I asked, "How about a pack of Luckys?"

She took my thirty-five cents and returned with the cigarettes. "See ya tomorrow," she said.

I left and walked down Broadway. It was already getting hot. The short fat cop was a few blocks down the street with his trustee, emptying pennies from parking meters. Broadway was also US highway 10 and traffic was steady. I studied the cars and trucks that went by. I liked cars and prided myself in being able to identify them. I watched for my favorites. A new 1955 Chevy hard top convertible, two-tone lemon and white passed by. I envied it, but knew I could never afford one. What I wanted was a 1949 Ford convertible, leaded-in and lowered like one I saw a kid from California driving. Maybe someday I could get one. If I hadn't spent all my money I could have already bought a 1941 Chevy coupe that sat in the used car lot across the street from Nona's café. It ran and cost only fifty dollars. I just had to save my money. But I wanted to look good when I started a new school, so what money I didn't piddle away went for clothes.

I turned and walked across the fill. This was Division Street, filled in across a quarter-mile horn of Moses Lake, with a wooden bridge in the middle. The lake was still and blue with green on the other side where willow trees lined the shore, and smooth lawns flowed from nice houses down to the lapping cool water.

I started daydreaming. Someday I would have my own house. It certainly wouldn't be a trailer house. I wanted a house with a nice green lawn and big trees, and enough bedrooms for everyone. Then I thought about joining the army and wearing a green uniform with ribbons on my chest. Moses Lake was full of airmen from Larson Air force Base, but their uniforms were plain looking. I heard someone say they looked like bus drivers. Occasionally some of them hung around the café early in the morning eating and sobering up. Who wants to join the Air Force and spend the whole time in Moses Lake? The army would send me to basic training in California, and everyone I knew thought California was the place to go.

On the far side of the lake I turned on to Stratford Road. It was getting hotter and the loose gravel was hard to walk on. My dreams faded as heat and fatigue brought me back to the task of walking home. The combination of working all night and sleeping in the daytime left me perpetually fatigued.

A few weeks earlier Bill had approached me and asked, "How would you like to earn some money?"

"Doing what?"

"We need a graveyard dishwasher at the café. It pays union wages," he said enthusiastically, trying to make it sound like a real good job.

"Okay, I'll do it," I agreed. That night at midnight I started my first real job, a job with a weekly paycheck. I felt important. But, now I was tired of it. I felt like a zombie. Trudging through the heat I told myself, *I'm quitting. I can't work when school starts, anyway.*

I reached highway 11-G and crossed over into

Black's Addition, a community of cheap houses, trailer houses, diseased Dutch Elm trees and lots of dogs. When I got home Mom and Bill were there. I announced my decision to quit working.

Bill said, "Can you come in Saturday and wash windows?"

I said, "yes" and that was all there was to it.

I went outside behind the trailer and stretched out on the bunk I had set up for day sleeping. It felt so good to lie down. I relaxed in the warm shade, listening to the sounds of birds and distant cars. While I lay waiting for sleep I thought about being a man. At sixteen, my childhood was over, but I wasn't a man yet either, but oh how I wanted to be grown up and be free to go my own way. I already proved that I could hold a real job. Now all I had to do was wait until I was a little older and I could strike out on my own. Too many moves and too many schools ruined my education. Every time we moved I fell further behind until I was held back two years. I knew I would never graduate. I'd have to be in school till I was twenty-years-old to do that. So school was just a place to socialize and wait. This isn't how I wanted things to be.

I thought about my mother. She grew up on a Minnesota homestead where she was treated with the cruelty of a slave. She could have been bitter, but instead she was kind and compassionate. She wanted to protect me from the hardships of life. Her childhood had been robbed from her, so she did what she could to see that I had all of what she never did. Many times

I heard her say, "You have only one childhood, you should enjoy it."

Well, I did enjoy it

When Grandpa Was a Kid

Chapter 2

The Farms and Forests of Home

In the spring of 1939 the Great Lakes generated one of its late season storms dumping snow on the farms and forests of Northern Minnesota. Grandma Strand's farmhouse stood alone in the deep new snow. Only the yellow lamplight glowing from the kitchen window separated it from the dark cold of night. Then came the cry of a newborn baby.

Doctor Pomelroy had arrived the night before. The snow was too deep for his car, so the Carlton County snowplow brought him to the farm. He rested on Grandma's bed upstairs, while Grandma and Dad watched over Mom, waiting for my arrival. My eight-year-old sister, Mavis, was there with them. Dad stuffed the stoves with wood to keep the house warm through the night. A small bed was set up in the corner of the kitchen for Mom but it was too soft, so the doctor shoved a legless ironing board under her to make his work easier. On the back of the stove stood a large pot of boiling water for the doctor to use. It was 2:10 a.m. on the 26th of April 1939 when Mom issued me into the world. My bassinet was an orange-crate with homemade wooden legs. Mom added a mattress and ruffles. I was eventually laid in my bed next to the warm cook stove. I like to tell people I was born on an ironing board and incubated in an orange-crate.

When Mavis was born, her bassinet was a dynamite box with a mattress made from cattail down.

When Grandpa Was a Kid

When Dad was born he also lay near a cook stove, even though it was the first full day of the summer of 1904. He was premature, weighing only four pounds and needed consistent heat. Grandma said he was too small to carry a middle name, so she named him just Clifford Strand. I was plenty big enough and was given the full name, Paul Clifford Strand.

Grandma's farm was a homestead granted to my Grandfather, Alexander Strand, in 1912 for $85.75. He cleared it, added a large barn and workshop, dug wells and built the house I was born in, with the help of his two sons, Alan and Clifford. He was from Norway and captained ships on the Great Lakes. Grandma was from Canada. They had five children, Alan, Clifford, Bertha, Florence and Jesse. Alan died of the Swine flu in 1918, alone in his room and away from home. He had been working in a sawmill in Cloquet, only a few miles from home. He was only fifteen. Grandpa died of pneumonia in 1929 at age 65, still developing his farm.

One of Minnesota's colorful nicknames is, The Land of Ten Thousand Lakes. This is an understatement because Minnesota has more than 15,000 lakes. You can add to that a lot of swamps, marshes and plenty of rivers, including the birthplace of the Mississippi. Most of the swamps and forests are in the north, west of Lake Superior and the city of Duluth. Grandma's farm was south west of Duluth near the town of Sawyer and a big lake called Big Lake.

Just beyond the farm and some swampy woods, was my other Grandparent's farm. Oscar and Hilda

The Farms and Forests of Home

Landgren were also homesteaders. They came from Sweden. Grandpa Landgren was thought to have left Sweden to escape the law. His real name was Oscar Olson. These were mom's stepparents.

Mom entered Ellis Island with the name Betty Mary Viola Falk. I guess she was big enough for two middle names. Viola was a cryptogram of her birth mother's name, Oliva (Olive, in Swedish.) Her stepmother entered as Hilda Emelia Falk. Grandma Landgren's first husband, John Falk, was waiting for her in Superior, Wisconsin, but because of his alcoholism and other problems, Grandma soon left him. Shortly after that, John took his own life by blowing his head off with a stick of dynamite.

Grandma then met Oscar and moved to his homestead were they later married, and Oscar adopted Mom. Mom's stepmother was probably a relative, but she wasn't told who her Swedish relatives were.

Oscar was an evil man who ruled his farm with abusive punishment. He liked to call himself "King Oscar." He overworked and beat my mother, depriving her of friends, toys, medical care, and worse. When Mom was 18, she married my father and was free of Oscar's oppressive little kingdom.

In 1939, the great depression still had farm prices too low to live on, causing rural Americans to remain unemployed or to work for small wages. Grandma Strand's saving grace was her Homesteader's Pension. It kept her fed and clothed and sometimes us too. She had no electric or telephone bills to pay. Water was hand pumped, and heat was from wood, most of which she cut herself. The Landgren's farm was better off. They had electricity, and Grandpa had a full time job in Cloquet working for the Northwest Paper Company. He worked his farm around his job while Grandma Landgren worked full time obeying the dictates of King Oscar.

Our home was a one-room cabin Dad built on our twenty acres, in a grove of Canoe Birch trees, across from Grandma Strand's farm. Mom took good care of our little home, surrounding it with flowers and attracting birds. She made friends with a couple of chipmunks she called Maggie and Jigs, they walked right up to her for handouts. The inside was rich with doilies and other homemade decorations.

As I toddled around our little home I carried my own milk bottle. Baby bottle nipples were made to fit common bottles such as ketchup or syrup bottles. Mom picked a bottle, filled it with milk and stretched a nipple over it. She preferred a pint whisky bottle, because I could carry it around in my pocket and take a swig whenever I felt like it.

Mom and Dad tried to make me eat eggs. I didn't like them. Mavis told me they tried to trick me by mixing eggs in my milk bottle. I held my bottle up to the light and said, "egg phooey", and chucked it against the wall. They also tried mixing eggs into other things, but I didn't usually fall for it.

Dad was always doing something. He played his violin, chopped wood, sometimes cooked and sometimes played with me. On one of our adventures together, Dad took me to a tub full of water that sat on

The Farms and Forests of Home

a box behind our cabin. Dad had gathered some pieces of wood and carved a little boat with a paddle powered by a rubber band. He wound it up tight and handed to me to put in the water. It went round and round. Then we rewound it and did it all over again.

To help economically, Mom did housekeeping, farm labor, ironing and anything that would keep the wolf away from the door. One thing I saw her do was make crepe paper flowers and sell them. She worked and twisted the paper until she had a large bouquet of yellow, red, and orange poppies. Some of them decorated our home.

Dad farmed and did odd jobs. He also did a little violin playing and elbow bending at the Big Lake Tavern. For a while, he tended bar there and we lived in a small house next door.

The yard was under the authority of a giant white rooster. Mom thought it would peck my eyes out. I thought it would kill me. This rooster stood as tall as me. Its thick red comb hung over its tilted head, cocked to one side so one big eye stared straight at me. I ran yelling, "Momma, Momma" with the big chicken right behind me. Someone always chased it away. Then, when things had settled and I returned to my play, the evil rooster would slowly strut back into the yard. One day, the rooster didn't come into the yard. I waited for it, but to my relief it was gone. Dad probably arranged its disappearance.

Dad loved to hunt. The woods were thick and supported plenty of wildlife; moose, deer, ducks, geese, partridge, bear and even Timber Wolves. His skillful hunting provided us with plenty of meat. My favorite was partridge.

Dad liked to involve me in the things he did and I was a willing participant. On one occasion he took me bird hunting. Since I was just a little guy, my job was to walk on fallen logs and forest debris ahead of him. He reasoned that since I was so short, I could spot birds by looking under the brush and across the forest floor and swamp water. If I saw a bird I was to stop and point at it. Dad would see where I was pointing, and shoot the bird. I had to go ahead of him on logs surrounded by water. I was afraid of falling in, and said so. I also talked too much. My career as a bird dog lasted only one day.

Dad butchered his own meat, both wild and domestic. One morning we went to Grandma Strand's farm to butcher a chicken for our supper. I stood in the tall grass and watched the action. Dad chased a chicken around the barn until he finally grabbed it. He slapped its neck across a chopping block and removed its head with one stroke of his hatchet. The chicken jumped up with blood pumping from its carotid arteries and without looking, continued running around the barn. Part way around it fell over.

Grandma Strand's farm

The Farms and Forests of Home

Dad picked it up and carried it to a bucket of steaming, hot water and dipped it in. Boiling water releases the feathers so they can be easily pulled out. He plucked the chicken and went into the house. Supper, for me, would be a fried drumstick.

Besides chickens, the farm had a horse, a cow, a dog and some cats. All were well cared for except the cats. They made their living killing mice in the barn and fields. One Christmas, Dad presented my cousin Sharon and me with mittens and parkas trimmed with white fur from some unlucky white cats.

When the hay was ready to cut, Dad hooked the horse to a rusty metal machine called a mower that the horse pulled through the field. A long arm protruded from its side like the business end of a barber's clipper and cut the hay. Dad sat on a metal seat with reins in his hands, sometimes with me on his lap. After the hay was cut, the horse dragged a big rake that pulled the cut hay into rows. The rows were pulled into piles and stacked by hand with pitchforks. When the fields were dotted with haystacks, my dad and anyone who was available pitched the hay onto a horse drawn wagon. Someone on the wagon caught the hay and arranged it until the load was quite high. A full wagon was pulled to the barn where the hay was picked up by a large set of hooks and lifted into the haymow.

At other times of year the horse pulled a plow and I could walk along and watch the earth roll away from the plowshare, while Dad's sturdy hands guided it across the field. To me the horse was a gentle monster in grey and white. Sometimes Dad would put me on

When Grandpa Was a Kid

its back to ride in from the field. My feet stuck straight out in front of me. It was soft and warm.

Similar things happened at the Landgren farm, where my mom grew up. It was only a mile or so through the swampy woods. Grandpa Landgren not only had horses and cows, he also had a tractor. The food was different too. Grandpa used to bake a tall pile of Swedish hard tack and set it out to dry. Grandma Landgren made sour cream butter. I watched the whole process. Fresh milk was put into a hand-cranked separator; centrifugal force sent the lighter cream out one tube, and the heaver milk out another tube. Grandma put the sour cream culture, which she had brought from Sweden, into the fresh cream and waited for it to sour. When the cream was ready, it was poured into a small wooden barrel churn and hand-cranked until butter was formed. Grandma poured out the buttermilk, and then worked the butter with a wooden paddle, forcing out the last drops of buttermilk and adding salt until it was solid pure butter, about two pounds.

Mavis before going west

They ate lots of sunfish that Grandpa caught in Big Lake. Fried fish, boiled potatoes, creamed spinach and grandpa's hardtack with grandma's sour cream butter made a delicious meal. Grandpa liked to eat

The Farms and Forests of Home

fried fish heads washed down with sour cream buttermilk. I stared with amazement and he grinned back.

There was one farm visible from Grandma Strand's place -- neighbors that were also friends. Mom and Dad took me along to a Christmas party at their house. Several guests filled the chairs and I was left to wander around. I wanted to drink what they were drinking, so I asked Mom, "Can I have some?"

"Okay, just a little sip." She handed me her beer glass and I tasted the contents.

Then I went to Dad. "Can I have a little sip?"

"Okay, but just a taste." He said.

Then I went to someone else, "Can I have a little taste?

And so I went around the room.

Then I looked up to the top of a treadle sewing machine where a small glass with beautiful amber liquid sat. I reached up and took it. It burned my mouth a little so I took just a taste, then just a sip. When it was gone I ran around the room laughing and giggling and stumbling to the floor. I shot out the door and jumped into a snow bank. I rolled and laughed. Mom grabbed me out of the bitter cold and carried me back into the house. It was now clear to everyone what had happened. I was drunk. My head was shoved under a cold stream of water. Mom also rammed my head into the faucet. Now I was in pain and the fun was gone. I screamed and screamed until my parents took me home.

I have many fond memories of home; like Dad's

When Grandpa Was a Kid

old flat bed Ford truck, whining its way up the driveway, Moms bicycle with me seated on the crossbar as we rode to the mail box, wolves howling in the night with the knowledge that everyone was home safe, Dad eating with dirty hands and telling his mother that dirt was good for you, Grandma Strand dragging a Christmas tree across the field from the forest and the belief that Santa Claus really left those sled tracks Dad made in the field. My earliest memory is the Northern Lights. Riding on my mother's lap, I looked up past my dad at the beautiful lights in the sky above a stretch of swamp water. I was about a year and a half old.

When World War II started everything changed. Mom and Aunt Jesse went to work in town and my cousin Sharon and I started spending time with Grandma Strand. We were about the same age and were treated alike. We became constant companions.

Grandma Strand, Mavis and Paul on the farm 1944

The Christmas of 1943 Sharon and I were each given a doll that we proudly held in our white cat fir mittens and fur trimmed parkas. Soon after, Dad left for Seattle to work in the war factories. Mom planned to take Mavis and me to

The Farms and Forests of Home

Seattle later to join him. There was finally money to be made and futures to plan.

Mom and Aunt Jesse worked in Duluth and only came home on weekends. Then Mom, Mavis and I would be together. One of those weekend nights, I was staying at the Landgren farm while Mom went out with friends. There was just Grandma and I alone on the farm, Grandpa was off doing something on his own. I stood in the window and watched as a red glow grew in the sky beyond the treetops. How could I know that our little house was burning down?

The next day we looked at a pile of ashes. Nothing remained. Farther back in the woods, were the ashes of an older cabin Dad built when he and Mom got married. It too burned in the night years earlier under mysterious circumstances. Who or what had burned both cabins? I was too young to know the heart ache my family suffered. They lost everything. I was happy to see that my peddle car safe in the yard. Everything else was gone

Paul on Grandma Strand's farm

With our little home in ashes Mavis and I moved in full time with Grandma Strand. I learned things by watching Grandma's constant industry. She baked bread once a week, planted a huge garden in the summer, canned fruit and vegetables for winter, chopped most of her own firewood, did laundry by hand, sewed clothing, made choke cherry wine and cared for Mavis, Sharon and me.

Mavis' school bus driver was also our milkman. In the cold of winter, grandma sent Sharon and me to meet the bus and get the milk. We each carried a quart bottle through the snow. It was so cold the cream on top froze and pushed the caps way up. Grandma cut the frozen cream off the top and put it in two dishes with sugar on top, and gave us each, "ice cream."

On snowy nights the wolves howled and we heard stories of how the wolves would circle cattle or even a person when winter food became scarce. Fear of wolves was part of my training. I was told stories about wolf attacks. Dad once told me he lay on the snow while wolves circled him. He had a rifle with him and shot one. The rest ran off. Another time a wolf chased him onto the porch. To further my fear of wolves Grandma caught me taking a leak in the yard and said, "If a wolf sees you doing that he'll come and bite that thing off."

With the thought of wolves lurking around, I behaved better most of the time.

On stormy nights, when the narrow two-story house shook in the wind, Grandma would bring Sharon and me downstairs. She made a comfy bed for us on the kitchen table with pillows and blankets. She would sit in a chair next to the table until the storm passed, just in case she had to whisk us to safety in the cellar below the kitchen.

My last Christmas in that simple farmhouse was

wonderful. Grandma cut a tree, all the grownups decorated it, food and drink were prepared, and candles were lit on the branches. Only the yellow lamplight glowing from the windows and the sound of Christmas carols separated it from the cold dark night.

When Grandpa Was a Kid

Chapter 3

Out West

Aunt Jessie loaded Mom, Mavis and me into her blue 1936 Ford coupe for our ride to the train station in Duluth. We were going out west to be with Dad, and I was ready to go. How was a five-year old boy supposed to know how far Seattle was from the swamps of northern Minnesota? How could I know that these places and people were disappearing from my life? I didn't even bother to put my paper soldiers away. They were scattered about the little bedroom upstairs in Grandma's house. I thought I could play with them again later.

In Duluth, we boarded a Union Pacific train. Our seats faced each other across a little table. The window was big giving us a wonderful view.

Our car jerked. We were on our way. Soon we were listening to the click and clack of the rail joints as we glided through the farms and forests. Suddenly, people rushed to the windows to see the Mississippi river as we crossed over. This part of the river wasn't much to look at. As the day passed, the forests diminished and farms spread across the open prairie. Soon Minnesota was behind us. Even though it was February, I saw huge haystacks in North Dakota and joked that they were the mountains that we were waiting to see.

The Second World War was raging in the Pacific and the train was packed with service men heading west, young men having fun, not knowing what was ahead for them. They were required to wear their uniforms and uniformed men were everywhere. I felt a kinship with these brave men, because I had a sailor suit in my luggage. Several walked through the aisles talking to each other. A few came and sat with us ostensibly to play cards. What they really wanted to do was flirt with my thirteen-old sister Mavis. The soldiers came around a lot and were a happy bunch. They liked to talk and play cards.

There was no dining car, so our meals arrived in small white paper boxes that held sandwiches and I don't remember what else. I thought they were wonderful. Mom supplemented them with a few snacks she had stashed somewhere. Mom always liked to surprise me with little goodies. Between meals we played cards and talked. I was happy to look out the window.

At night the conductors converted the seats into beds. This was a Pullman car. Mavis got the top bunk and I crawled in with Mom on the bottom. Curtains covered the beds leaving just a narrow hallway. During the night we sped past the sounds and lights of crossing barriers and trains rushing the other direction.

On the morning of the third day we awoke to the long awaited mountains. The train curved below the peaks so that the two matching engines, pulling the train up the steep mountain grade, could be seen from our window. They poured heavy smoke as they strained along the narrow track cut into the almost vertical mountainside. Far below among boulders the size of trucks and houses, a thin stream of white water foamed past dark green trees. We were in the Cascade Mountains. We had slept through the Rockies.

On the evening of the third day we stepped off the train in the Union Station in Seattle. There was Dad standing tall and slim with a big smile under his thin black mustache. We gathered our bags and started through the covered station. The high roof trapped the steam and coal smoke, until it cooled and settled over the trains. Chugging engines, hissing steam, ringing bells, couplers striking couplers, voices and footsteps filled my ears. A war was on and Seattle was urgently busy.

Mavis and I sat in the back seat of Dad's big old Buick limousine and we all went home together, for the first time in two years.

We arrived in February of 1945. Americans were at war. Seattle was busy day and night; building bombers at Boeing, casting machinery at Bethlehem Steel, building ships in the Bremerton shipyards, sewing tents at Puget Sound Tent and Awning, building trucks at Kenworth, and fabricating rail cars at Pacific Car and Foundry. Business was booming and wages were good. Like my Dad did two years earlier, people poured in from all over the country to fill the new jobs. Housing became scarce.

Our small house sat on a flat hilltop on 176th Street South, between the federal highway 99 (Now International Boulevard) and Military Road, above the Kent Valley in the community of McMicken Heights. Dad built the house himself, but hadn't yet finished it.

Thin laths held a wrapping of tar paper to the outside walls and the roof was covered with split cedar shakes. On the inside were two small bedrooms, a little living room and a nook of a kitchen. There was no running water, no electricity, and no bathroom, just the usual outhouse, but fortunately, Dad knew carpentry and built our house to be strong and comfortable.

We got our water from a communal water faucet at the King County dump, a couple of miles away. This huge dump received garbage from all over the county. Mounds of garbage built up until a bulldozer pushed it off the edge, where it tumbled through flames to the Kent Valley below. At the bottom were pools of filthy water that seeped into the Green River.

The dump was always burning, sending up black smoke that could be seen for miles. It cast a red glow into the sky at night. The air around it stunk. Dad warned me not to walk anywhere near the edge because of the danger of falling into burned out cavities. "That's where the rats live," he said.

Near the entrance were some shacks mostly constructed from refuse. The black people who lived there cared for the dump and combed it for anything useful. All around the shacks were tall stacks of empty bottles, tires and other things that could be sold. While black clouds of smoke drifted above us, we filled our washtub and other containers with water and carefully drove home.

Houses like ours were common during the war, as the need for ships and airplanes left little resources for home building or public utilities. Our new home was

Out West

nothing like the remote solitude of Minnesota's forested swamps. Here we had paved roads, highways and towns. There were hills, mountains, rivers, valleys, Puget Sound and its islands. It seldom got hot or cold but it rained a lot. It drizzled, showered, sprinkled, poured and fogged.

When Grandpa Was a Kid

Chapter 4

Bow Lake

Our new neighborhood had plenty of kids my age. There were two boys named Gary, one lived at the top of the hill and the other lived at the bottom of the hill. They became known as hilltop Gary and hollow Gary. I got to know hollow Gary pretty well, but I was afraid of hilltop Gary's Doberman Pincer and avoided going near his house.

The nicest house on our street belonged to The Kennedys. It was a white steep roofed house of late thirties design. It had a separate dining room with polished furniture and a fireplace in the living room. The mother was kind to her little boy's friends. Her husband was off leading men in the Pacific war. One more thing set them apart; they owned a small restaurant on Highway 99 made out of a giant redwood stump that was hauled in pieces from California and reassembled with doors, windows and a kitchen.

Across from the Kennedy house was a small house filled with a family of seven. One kid was my age. The last time I visited him, his parents had left the kids home alone. During their absence, kids jumped on the furniture and played like wild people tracking mud through the open front door. This unsettled me because I was trained never to play on the furniture or dirty the house. But before I could leave, the parents returned. They didn't like what they saw and lined us up and give each of us a spanking. I never returned to that house.

A few blocks away was a new housing development of two and three bedroom houses. Though small, they looked nice with lawns and sidewalks. Just a few blocks into the new neighborhood was a Quonset hut occupied by a small grocery store. Groceries could be picked off the shelves by the shopper and paid for at a counter. Mom brought along her own bags, egg carton, and returnable bottles. Because of the war, we could only buy what our limited supply of ration stamps would allow. No stamps meant no sugar, meat or coffee. And there were never enough stamps. I remember my mom saying sugar was scarce, so she learned to drink her coffee black, but Dad drank tea with sugar and canned milk.

Mom brought home a cat she named Tinka. It was a nice cat and I began to learn something about how cats behave. To show me how cats are instinctual, Dad placed Tinka on the top rung of a wooden ladder leaning against the house. He repeatedly instructed her how to climb down the ladder backward, but the cat always tried to come down head first. She demonstrated some more instinctual behavior when Mom opened the door and threw a long narrow stream of coffee grounds across the yard. They struck Tinka under her tail and up she leaped. I watched in amazement, as the cat smelled the long trail of coffee grounds leading to the door. Then, she carefully buried the whole stream, sat down, and contentedly cleaned herself.

Another cat training incident got me in enough trouble to get spanked. At the end of street, on the corner of 176th and Highway 99 was a small combination gas station and grocery store. The owners, Leo and Connie Unrue, were family friends. They lived in an apartment attached to the rear of the business. Sometimes when we visited, I went out alone to play beside the station. On one such occasion I found the Unrue's kitten happily rolling around in the dirt.

In those days flat tires were common. To find the leak in the inner tube, the tube was filled with air and pushed into a half tire shaped trough of water. Bubbles rose from the leak showing the mechanic where to apply a patch. A full trough of water sat behind the station. I thought it would be a good idea to teach the dusty kitten how to swim. I put a narrow board across the trough and placed the kitten in the center. The kitten should fall off when I turned the board over, and then I could help it learn to swim. As soon as the kitten was on the board it started meowing. I rotated the board, but the thing didn't fall in, instead it dug in its claws and hung with its back in the water trying to pull itself up. It made a terrible noise. Just as I was trying to push my reluctant student into the water, my dad showed up to see what was going on. He grabbed the kitten from the water then turned me over his knee.

When Grandpa Was a Kid

Dad's car was a big black 1933 Buick limousine. He used it to pull a trailer for hauling building materials for our house. I loved that car. It had a huge back seat with two jump seats that could be folded down for extra seating. I usually had the whole back seat to myself, because Mavis was at school. But one night we were all together on a rainy road, when Dad failed to stop at an intersection. He hit a car. Off we went with the victim in hot pursuit. Dad had broadsided Sheriff Callahan. He chased us through White Center and West Seattle while Mom and Mavis yelled at my desperate father. What a ride. We finally ditched him. Unfortunately for Dad, the sheriff had our license number and Dad eventually had to settle with the court.

Paul on his dad's 1933 Buick

One afternoon in another intersection, this time in downtown Seattle, a large Boeing delivery truck flopped on its side right in front of us. It had been hit hard, broadside. Dad leaped from the car and climbed up onto the truck. He pulled the passenger door open and lifted the driver to safety. My Dad could outrun cops and save injured motorists, just like in the movies.

The downside of riding around with Mom and

Bow Lake

Dad was the emergency "pee" can Mom made me keep. Another insult was Mom's hanky. She would spit on it and clean spots off my face before we went into places.

At home, Dad liked to tease Mavis. I thought it was fun too. She loved to listen to Frank Sinatra. She'd stand there and say things like, "He's a dream boat."

That caused Dad to call him Frank Snot Rag. It got so bad that Mavis cried at the insult. I didn't like Snot Rag either. I liked Bing Crosby. He sang songs like, "Would you like to Swing on a star?" and, "Ac-cent-tchu-ate the positive." Who cared about Sinatra singing, "Embrace me, my sweet embraceable you."

"Oh Frankie," Mavis swooned.

Yuck! Sometimes I'd tease her too. I called her my big "sis-turd". She called me her little bother.

Mavis developed an ingrown toenail. It got infected and turned into blood poisoning. Surgery and bed rest followed. She missed several days of school. Mavis and I were home alone when the Highline School District nurse arrived. I was putting Cheerios wheels on toothpick axles to mobilize a modeling clay car, when she knocked. I opened the door and in barged the Highline school nurse Gondaufle. She went straight to Mavis' bed and inspected her toe. The nurse concluded the toe was fine, then belittled her for staying home, ordering her to get out of bed and go to school. Mavis refused. When Dad heard of this he was furious. The nurse's nickname around school was nurse God-awful.

When Grandpa Was a Kid

I had my brush with doctors when I stood behind my friend who swung an axe that we were forbidden to touch. On the backswing he hit me square in the mouth with the blunt end. I ran in the house screaming and spewing blood from my mouth and terrifying the family. I was rushed to the Renton General Hospital with no broken teeth or bones but a badly swollen and discolored cheek

Both Mom and Dad worked. Dad had a few jobs including brakeman on the Milwaukee Railroad, and, after that, was with Cunningham Steel until the end of the war. Mom took catalogue orders for Sears Roebuck at their big downtown building.

Sometimes on Saturday Mom would take me shopping in Seattle. We would board one of the Greyhound buses that ran between Seattle and Tacoma every few minutes, sometimes traveling two buses together. They were usually full and we often had to stand in the aisles. In Seattle, we would go to Kress's and Woolworth's on opposite corners of Third and Pine, and if we needed clothes we went to Penney's on Second Avenue where its many stories took up an entire city block. Lunch was at Kress or better yet a second story cafeteria nearby called Manning's. It was my favorite place to have lunch with Mom. On a cold day it was so warm in there, and it smelled heavenly. I ate shimmering Jell-O cubes with whipped cream on top while we sat in a window booth and watched the busy street below.

Although trips to Seattle were always fun, my favorite time was Christmas, when we saw the

Bow Lake

elaborate Christmas displays with electric trains running through villages and mountains, even layers of trains with trestles. One window had Santa and his mechanized elves getting ready for Christmas. Music filled the stores and the streets. On a corner an odd little brass band played Christmas music. Lights were everywhere. It was so beautiful. I didn't want it to end, so Mom lovingly led me back to the better displays for a second look.

Mom loved movies and she picked movies I liked. We would go to the Blue Mouse, 5th Avenue, or my favorite, the Paramount with its stack of balconies and huge chandeliers. The newsreel was always about the war, followed by previews, a cartoon, and then the main feature, often a double feature. In the dark, I could hear Mom rustling around in her full shopping bag for treats. She knew I loved chocolate and would slip me a Hershey bar, or sometimes a cookie.

Stepping into the street during the war could mean darkness. Seattle wasn't usually blacked out, but it was ready for blackout at a moment's notice. Our bus passed through the Boeing Company in South Seattle. We could see majestic B-29 bombers and factory buildings, some with their doors open to the production inside. But none of this could be seen from the air. The entire Boeing factory was covered with netting painted to look like streets. Even fake houses and trees were constructed. From the air it looked like a typical blacked-out neighborhood.

On the other side of Highway 99 from our neighborhood, was the high forested ground of

When Grandpa Was a Kid

Highline Ridge. On it was the small and unfinished Bow Lake Field. It was started before the war. Now it was being built into a real airport to be called SeaTac. I stood on the hill beyond Hollow Gary's house and watched bulldozers push the fallen forest into huge piles to be burned. SeaTac airport was being created. It didn't take long either. In a few months, military planes would be landing and taking off.

From this hill I sometimes waited for Mom to get off the bus from work. I could meet her and walk home holding my mother's hand. She was often tired and sick.

As I played in the yard one August afternoon, Two P-47 Thunderbolts climbed high in the sky above our house. Then down they came, full speed, then pulled up with a great whine and a loud roar as they pulled back up to the heavens to do it all over again. Mavis came out of the house to watch. She said the radio had just announced the end of World War II.

Soon after the surrender, Bow Lake Airport had an open house to show off warplanes. Fighters and bombers were parked and ready for our inspection. I got to see inside a shiny black P-38 Lightning and some other shiny new fighter planes, thus solidifying a lifelong love of World War II airplanes.

I was soon enrolled in the Angle Lake Grade School -- first grade. The young and lovely Miss Kurtz greeted us. We were seated two to a table. I was thrilled to be in school, but some of the other kids started crying when their mothers left them. My very first school assignment was to learn to print my name on a card and have it taped to the corner of my desk. School was learning to read from my Dick and Jane book, drawing with crayons, being in reading circles, and taking naps. Miss Kurtz always smiled.

One day a week, I could buy an ice cream bar from our principal who stood in the school yard with a big cardboard box full them. A cloud of mist covered the frozen treats inside. They only cost a nickel. Our principal was also my bus driver. On busy roads he stopped to let kids off, then got out and held a cloth stop sign on a long steel rod. One night on the way home a car didn't stop for his sign, so he brought the rod down hard on the trunk of the car hard enough to leave a crease. The car kept on going, while us kids cheered for our principal.

My stop was on the corner of Military road and 176th Street under the long limbs of a tall Big Leaf Maple tree. My walk home was about three quarters of a mile. Hill Top Gary walked on one side of the road, and I on the other. On an otherwise lovely day, a bolt of lightning struck the crown of the road between us.

"Wow, did you see that?" I yelled

"I'm getting out of here!" Gary yelled back.

We both ran home, safe but scared. After that I never walked along the crown of a road.

But my greater fear was a small dog that came out every night to bark at us as we walked up the same street. I never knew when he would attack. Living near wolves had given me an unnatural fear of dogs.

Soon we were listening to Christmas music on the radio and opening gifts. We had a box of Whitman's

Samplers, too. Dad gave me a bow that he carved from a piece of western yew, and some arrows he made from cedar.

That winter I began to get earaches. They got worse. Dad used to comfort me by blowing warm cigarette smoke into my ear. Before long I was in bed with a high fever from tonsillitis. I hallucinated. The corners of the room appeared to stretch up into the clouds as they rippled and curled. When Mom came to comfort me, I never saw her. Instead I saw a huge terrible monster. I screamed for the beast to get away from me and yelled, "Momma help me, Where are you?"

On the nightstand was a bottle of Cocoadiazine, a chocolate flavored sulpha, provided by the doctor at the Renton General Hospital. It helped fight the infection and I loved the taste. The sulfa worked and the fever passed.

Mom changed jobs. She started cooking for the Black Ball Ferry Line. She alternated between the Willapa, Enetai and Kalakala ferry boats. The Kalakala was once a ferry named Peralta. A fire in 1933 nearly destroyed it. After that, it was towed from the San Francisco Bay to Seattle, where it was transformed into the world's first streamlined ferry. Its Art Deco style shined with polished aluminum. Mom loved working on this graceful boat, and talked about it for years afterward. The other two boats were moved to Puget Sound from San Francisco after the Golden Gate Bridge put them out of business in the late 1930s. They too were refitted and renamed. All three were assigned the Seattle to Bremerton run.

Mom's new job caused some problems. She didn't drive and had to be near the docks to get to and from her job. Mom also worked odd hours. I don't know what other reasons there may have been, but she took a room in a house in West Seattle to be near her job. She could ride the Seattle Transit electric trolleys to and from work.

I had to have my tonsils out. Mom found out that the Red Cross would perform the operation without cost. But I would have to stay with her at her apartment while I recovered from surgery. To prepare me for the operation Mom promised me all the ice cream and Jell-O I wanted and said I could lie around and listen to the radio and read comic books for a couple of days until I was healed. No big deal.

The Red Cross Operatorium was one big room with beds and draw curtains. It was tonsillectomy day. I was put on a bed and prepared for my operation, which came fast. I was put on a gurney and moved to another part of the room. A curtain was drawn around me. A nurse poured chloroform on a cloth and forced it over my mouth and nose. I struggled but my arms and legs were tied down. I was losing consciousness and fighting against it. Then they pinched me hard to see if I was still awake. I tried to scream.

Then I was back on my bed throwing up through my mouth and nose. Blood and vomit shot into a big pan. I was groggy and coughing up with burning pain. After a while I settled down to just bleeding and groaning. What had they done? It hurt to swallow. It hurt to breathe. My head pounded and I was sick. Mom got me dressed and we went out to a taxi and back to Mom's room.

I lay in Mom's bed unable to eat, read comics or listen to the radio. Mom coaxed me to just drink some water. She apologized profusely. After a couple of days the bleeding stopped and I began to eat some ice cream. I soon healed. For a long time food kept coming out of my nose. They had taken my adenoids too.

As soon as I was well, Mom took me to a movie and did some other nice things for me, then returned me home to be with Dad and Mavis and return to school. I saw Mom when she came home on her days off.

Because of tonsillitis, I missed a lot of school. I can't remember how the rest of that spring went, but I do remember some people coming to look at our house. We were getting ready to move.

Chapter 5

The Forty-acre Forest

The war was over and Dad's last employer, Cunningham Steel, was shut down. Dad wasn't looking for a new job. Instead he made a deal to exchange our home in McMicken Heights for forty acres of timber in Southwest Washington. The forested land would be a place to rebuild some of the life left behind in Minnesota. Dad would sell off the timber and build Mom a log house. Mom would use her artistic talents to paint wild life murals on its living room walls.

When moving day came, Mavis and I climbed into the back of the Buick. Our belongings were in the car and stacked high on a large flat trailer. The same trailer Dad had used to haul in the materials for the construction of our home that disappeared behind us. We turned south on Highway 99.

Highway 99 was a modern highway completed only a few years earlier. It stretched from Canada to Mexico. The original, but smaller, Highway 99 was completed in 1915. Because the federal government built it, it was also called the Federal Highway, providing a name to the small community of Federal Way, just north of Tacoma. The Federal Highway had some other names too. But because it covered over much of an older highway called the Pacific Coast Highway, it was called Pacific Highway South, south of Seattle, and Pacific Avenue in Tacoma. The Pacific

Coast Highway was the first west coast highway with pavement; it replaced the Military road which was originally a dirt road from San Francisco to Canada, and it also covered some other shorter runs of road. These roads had their beginnings in Indian trails. Successive highways replaced earlier ones, leaving remnants of the old highways and roads behind, like ox bows on a river plain.

We went through Tacoma, Tenino, Centralia and Chehalis, where we left Highway 99 and turned onto the old Pacific Highway continuing south toward Napavine and beyond, toward our destination.

Somewhere along the way we stopped for gas. Everyone but me, laughed and joked about the gas station price sign. It took me a long time to catch on to the meaning of, "Ethel 5 gals for a dollar."

We turned off the paved roads beyond Napavine and followed gravel roads to a narrow dirt road, and finally a narrow rutted drive into our property. We stopped in a flat, grass covered, clearing surrounded by tall trees. There we were, alone in the forest ready to start our new home from scratch.

It was late afternoon and we had no shelter. Everyone but me went to work on a platform for our room sized, war surplus tent. When night came, I crawled onto the trailer and found a pile of something soft and curled up under a quilt. I thought about all the changes in our lives, but I fell asleep looking forward to the great adventure of exploring this new forest.

In the morning the tent was done, our iron cook

The Forty-acre Forest

stove sat in front of it, and the tub we used for hauling water from the dump sat on a stump. Even our wooden icebox had a place. Mom loved the forest and would make do with what we had. After all, a house would be built. As tired as she was, she had bacon and eggs with coffee ready for breakfast. I was offered canned milk, which I promptly turned down.

That same day, I had the pleasure of watching my dad begin work on a cabin to be made almost exclusively from what the forest could provide. He started right in the middle of our clearing. Small fir logs were cut and used for floor joists carefully positioned on rocks. A frame of maybe 12' X 14' feet defined its size. Boards were nailed down to make a floor. The forest was combed for matching slender fir trees with four-inch diameters. These poles were limbed and barked, then cut and trimmed. Dad built the entire framework using these poles. Some of them were split and attached horizontally to receive cedar shakes. A doorframe was constructed and a small window installed.

Not far from our clearing was an old fallen Western Red Cedar. With his big crosscut saw, Dad cut it into rounds of maybe eighteen or 24 inches. The rounds were split into blocks, called bolts, which were as wide as the desired shakes. Dad placed a shake cutting knife, called a froe, on the cedar bolt, at the desired thickness of a shake, and struck it with a mallet. A shake popped off the bolt. Dad cut enough shakes to cover the entire cabin, sides and roof.

On the inside, a board counter was prepared, and

a pair of wooden orange crates was hung on the wall for cupboards. Within a few days the cabin was complete. It had the heavenly aroma of freshly cut cedar.

Most of the cutting and fitting was done with Dad's razor sharp axe, yielding plenty of scraps and chips. I was given the job of collecting the excess for firewood and kindling.

There was plenty for a seven-year-old boy to do. I wandered in the trees, played at the pond and stayed close to my dad. Thus began our summer of 1946.

On one edge of the clearing, stood a thick limbless snag. Dad estimated it to be 100 feet tall. At the top were bees. Where there are bees there is honey. The snag was unstable and had to come down. The three of us stood at a safe distance while Dad cut into the trunk. The snag slowly tilted. Dad ran off to one side as the tree began to fall. It hit flat on the ground shattering from end to end and shaking our feet. The bee's nest splashed like a big yellow watermelon. Bees filled the air as they swarmed around the remains of their nest. Eventually they dispersed and we could approach the mess. There was lots of honey, but it was mixed with rotten wood, bee's wax, dead bees and their larva. It was splattered for several feet. The honey was ruined. But it was good that the snag was down as it could have fallen at any time, damaging more than just a bee's nest.

Throughout the property were the stumps of ancient Douglas fir trees. They were thick high stumps with little holes chopped into the sides, which Dad said were springboard holes. He explained that the tree fallers had to get high enough up the tree to cut above the wide bottom part of the trunk, so they cut notches and wedged in boards to stand on while they worked. The biggest stumps had springboards for climbing up to the working level springboards. To fell one of these giants first required judging where the tree would land. Then, because of its size, a cradle of smaller trees was arranged to catch the big tree and prevent it from cracking or splintering. The tree was notch cut with axes, one man on each side alternating their swing as they cut into the wide trunk. Once the notch was cut they moved to the other side of the tree, and began cutting with a long crosscut saw they liked to call a "misery whip". They stood way out on their springboards and pulled the saw back and forth against the tree. They never pushed.

My imagination soared as Dad explained how one of these monsters fell. When the cutting was done, steel wedges were driven into the saw cut, forcing the tree to tilt in the planned direction. Then the cutters would yell, "timber" and jump from the springboards and run to a safe place. The tree tilted slowly at first, then made a cracking sound as it broke free of the stump. It started its descent in a leisurely manner, and then speeded up until the air rushed through its branches and it crashed heavily into its cradle. Broken branches, bits of needles and dust followed it down. When it was still, loggers moved in to cut off the branches and cut the tree into transportable logs. Felling one of these trees could take a couple of days or more, with the hand tools they used at the time. When I eventually saw one of these giants fall, it was just like dad explained. I thought if Dad had made a cradle for the snag we wouldn't have lost all that honey

Because our land had been partially logged several years earlier, pathways remained in the woods giving us easy access to most of the forty-acres. But one trail was different. Rotten logs lay across the marshy road that once supported wagons as they were pulled across the wet ground. Dad called it a corduroy road. He said this was the remains of the old Military Road that was built back when the United States wanted to move troops from San Francisco to fight the British over the border between the US and Canada.

Along the trails were rotting stumps with red huckleberry bushes growing in them. One morning I was handed a coffee can and told to go fill it with huckleberries. I didn't quite fill the can, but Dad was happy. I watched him roll out dough and lay it in a pie tin, add berries and sugar, top it with another layer of dough, trim it, poke holes in it, paint it with butter and sugar, then stick it in the oven. A hot wood fire baked the pie, as smoke rose from the short stovepipe. The smell of burning wood and baking pie filled the clearing. Dad cut the little pie in two and we each ate half.

On another morning, Dad took an old Borden's condensed milk can; cleaned off the paper, cut off the ends with a tin snip, then cut the remainder into pieces. He soldered everything together, and handed me a toy plow. I dragged it through the ground and watched the earth curl away from the plowshare, just like the real one did back on the farm in Minnesota. After a couple of days my little treasure disappeared. Everyone looked for it, but it was never found.

Across the road from our piece of forest was a dairy farm. It belonged to the Knokes family. The farm had a small house, a big barn, and fields of cows. Mr. And Mrs. Knokes had two grown daughters. One of them had a five-year-old girl, but no husband.

While we were visiting, one of their boyfriends showed up with a motorcycle. I asked for a ride. My request was granted. I sat behind the boyfriend and we were off, roaring down the gravel county road. When we reached the highway to Winlock, he turned back into our trail of dust and opened up the throttle for a thrilling ride back to the farm. When I jumped off, the five-year-old jumped on. She got a thrilling ride too.

This adventure later prompted Dad to tell me one of his not-so-verifiable stories. "When I was a young man," he began, "I sped down a gravel road on an Indian motorcycle. I lost control on a gravel covered wooden bridge and slid down the road on my hind end. I carried a pipe in my back pocket that was worn down into the bowl." Then he said, "You should have seen the other cheek."

This may have been Dad's way of scaring me away from motorcycles.

We were at the Knokes farm on the Fourth-of-July along with several people and plenty of food, beer, pop, and fireworks. Later that afternoon the five-year-old girl and I wandered away to our pond. I brought along some marshmallows to roast. I knew the dangers of fire in the forest, so I carefully cleaned off the ground next to the pond and placed a little stack of kindling in the center.

Then the young girl said, "Here's a better place for a fire."

Before I could stop her she had lit a small pile of cut brush. I tried to put it out by throwing pond water at it, but it quickly grew larger. We ran as fast as possible to the farmhouse yelling, "fire fire!"

Dad and Mister Knokes met us in the yard. By then, smoke was climbing above the trees. All the men at the party fought the fire the rest of the afternoon. By the time the fire was out, almost an acre was blackened. The men's clothes were ruined. I was questioned about the incident, but never got in trouble. I felt so terrible that no amount of punishment was needed.

Late one August evening, Dad and I were waiting for Mavis to come home from somewhere nearby – maybe the Knokes farm -- when the sky filled with shooting stars. I lay back in an inner tube watching the show, when suddenly meteors lighted the sky; one was so bright we could see our clearing just like day. Shortly after that, Mavis arrived. She said she was coming up the road through the dark woods when the sky lit up giving her a real scare. We spent the rest of the evening under the stars, but the show was over.

Our forty acres still had a good supply of native trees that Dad planned to harvest. But Dad's luck went

The Forty-acre Forest

bad. He was directing a load of material being backed into our clearing, when he was struck in the chest with a protruding board. I saw him fall. He broke some ribs. This laid him up for a time. He also got sick with tonsillitis and had to have his tonsils removed. These misfortunes put a stop to progress for the summer. Dad eventually healed, but some of his enthusiasm was gone, and so was summer.

Summer ended for me when I was enrolled in the two-room Eveline School. Each row of seats was a separate grade. Oddly, it had a gymnasium. School wasn't memorable, nor was much else until Halloween.

It was a gloomy, rainy Halloween. The cook stove was moved into the cabin, and dad was baking a pan of brownies for trick-or-treaters. It seemed strange to me that he expected trick-or-treaters to find our cabin. We left to pick up Mom and Mavis and were gone until sundown. Dad insisted we get back to the cabin, so we wouldn't miss the trick-or-treaters. When we got back, it was dark and cold. The tent hung with water, the driveway was muddy and everything was wet and clammy. There wasn't a trick-or–treater within a country mile.

Gone was the camp out atmosphere of summer living, with warm evenings and out-door adventures. That all disappeared with the onset of dark, wet fall weather. Our abysmal living conditions put an end to our stay in the forty-acre forest.

When Grandpa Was a Kid

Chapter 6

The Ancient Orchard

At seven years old I had no idea what squatter meant. But that's what we were – squatters. Dad found out about an old abandoned farm not far from our 40 acres of woods, just outside of Winlock

We moved in. It was the old Billy Walters place. Walters came from Germany in 1875 and found his way to Lewis County, Washington where he cleared his homestead and built a farm. He added a barn and several outbuildings, dug a well and planted apple trees, propagating his own varieties. His old trees still gave life where they surrounded the homestead and shaded the old buildings. A proud pioneer farm carved from the vast primeval forest of a new land.

By the time we moved in the barn lay flat on the ground, and mosses and lichens covered the sagging roofs of the remaining outbuildings. The boards on the front porch of the house were rounded and soft.

My dad warned us, "Be careful, the porch is slick when it's wet."

It couldn't have been slicker if it had been oiled.

It was a tall simple house with a covered porch and no remaining paint. It had three rooms downstairs; a front room, a kitchen, and a bedroom. Some old furniture was scattered about and an iron cook stove dominated the kitchen. The windows were narrow and went almost to the floor in every room. The floors were warped and sloping. There was no electricity or plumbing and the only water was from the hand dug well by the front porch. It had a little roof, crank, bucket, and a long rope. I could see the water far below, through the square hole in the wooden well cover.

A door opened to a narrow staircase that led up to a large landing where a single door opened to a small bedroom. Mavis claimed the bedroom for herself. I found a good corner of the landing. We settled in and slept our first night in this strange old house. At night we heard it shift and creak with age and I wondered if it was going to fall down. I was glad to have my sister nearby.

In the morning a hot fire warmed us, as bacon and eggs fried and coffee perked on the old cook stove. Soon the house was warm and filled with the familiar fragrance of breakfast mixed with smoke from the wood stove, and Dad's hand rolled cigarette.

Outside, the sky was a seamless dark cloud. A curl of smoke rose from the chimney and disappeared into the matching grey sky. It was also the time of year when storms pulled at the trees and threatened frail buildings.

After breakfast, the four of us explored the farm. We looked in several old buildings and sheds that once held chickens, horses and carriages. Now they too were ready to go the way of the barn. Around the sagging buildings were the ancient apple trees, their gnarled limbs covered with late season fruit. Many more apples lay rotting in the tall grass beneath the trees. The apples and the remaining fall leaves tinted

The Ancient Orchard

the trees with muted reds and yellows against a backdrop of the dark green forest beyond.

We walked among the apple trees marveling at the variety. Dad and Mom ventured names for them like Jonathan and Macintosh, but there were many more varieties that never had names. We sampled a few of them. They were red, yellow, green, large, small, hard and soft. One tree bore huge red apples neither sweet nor sour but juicy and crisp. Some were hard and tart.

"Cooking apples," Mom said.

Here we were, traipsing around on someone else's property when we had land of our own that we could no longer live on, only a few miles away, plus twenty more acres in Minnesota. But, plans and dreams weren't fulfilled. The problem was Dad didn't have a job. He told Mom once, back on the farm in Minnesota, "I'll never work for a boss." During World War II he had bosses, but the war had ended and he hadn't worked since.

So Mom found work as a waitress at the Saint Helens Hotel in Chehalis about 20 miles away, and stayed in town on days that she worked. Her wages paid for our food and Dad's gas. Dad stayed home and kept an eye on the place and us kids. He also did most of the cooking, which often included apples! We were served baked apples, applesauce, and pie. His favorite was baked apples covered with canned milk. I refused to eat them. To my mind, canned milk would ruin anything. Although Dad was a good cook, he had no interest in housekeeping. Mavis did most of the woodcutting, dishwashing and cleaning. Clothes were hand washed in a tub of hot water drawn from the well and heated on the cook stove. Mom pitched in when she was home. About all I did was shake out the rugs. I was busy enjoying my childhood.

I was enrolled in the second grade in the little town of Winlock, a mile and a half away. Winlock was the egg capital of the United States. They were in fact, the second largest egg producers in the United States. To prove it, the city erected a five-foot long plastic egg by the road, at the edge of town.

At school, my class was divided into five rows. Smart kids sat in a row called the Hummingbirds, over by the wall. Since I was new and untried, I sat in a row for dumb kids called the Busy Bees. Fortunately, my row was by the windows. I could at least visually escape from class while I waited to go home. There was another new boy in school. He was placed in the Hummingbirds row because he knew how to spell; a distinction that always separates people.

Our teacher was big on language. One day she was explaining poetry and rhyming. She read some poetry, and then explained that rhyming words, such as bake and cake or cat and bat, ended with the same sound.

It wasn't raining outside and I watched some older kids walking away from the school. I longed to do the same. Then the teacher said, "Who can rhyme two words in a sentence, how about you, Paul?"

I was stunned. I turned from the window to see everyone looking at me. I wished I could disappear.

The Ancient Orchard

"Go ahead, Paul, rhyme two words in a sentence."

I thought everyone could hear my heart beat, as I said, "The little bunny sprained his knee?" The class laughed. My position with the Busy Bees by the window was secure.

Being lumped in with the under achievers was a new and unwelcome experience that I would be forced to get used to in the years to come.

Recess was worth the whole experience. I found myself among kids who enjoyed cowboy heroes as much as I did. Best of all, the school allowed us to play with our cap guns. I had a pearl-handled .45 caliber Colt Peace Maker with a holster strapped to my leg. Fifteen minutes of shooting and ducking with the smell of cap gun smoke hanging in the air.

"Take that you dirty clod buster. Bang! Bang!"

"You're dead!"

"I am not!"

That fall, Dad's boyhood friend Jack Hanradi and his family arrived pulling a tiny trailer house, which they parked by our muddy driveway. They had three kids; Melva, a girl Mavis's age, another one named Mavis (of all names), and a boy named Larry, a couple of years older than me. All five of them were crammed into that tiny trailer and they planned to stay all winter. The kids enrolled in school, giving Mavis and me someone to walk to school with.

Jack didn't work either, but his family sure enlivened our social life. At night, Dad played the violin and Jack played the guitar. Mavis was trying to do something with a steel guitar. The kitchen sounded as good as it smelled. The fun was contagious. Plus, Mavis and I had new companions.

I went with Mavis to her steel guitar lessons. One guy knew what he was doing and played a tune for us, which sounded weird but nice. Everyone else sounded terrible including Mavis. Another time, Dad and I went with Mavis to watch a basketball game at the high school.

Although we had to abandon our cabin and tent in the forty-acre forest, the land was still ours, and Dad had it logged. One Sunday we went to see the logging. Trees had been felled, but not yet removed. Logs crossed logs. Some of these logs were quite large and I had fun walking on them, high over the brush. The tent and cabin were gone, but I knew my little plow was still there.

Paul in plaid coat with new scooter

Since Mom worked in Chehalis, I got to spend some time with her in town, where we went window-shopping. Just before Christmas, we stopped in front of a store window so I could stare at an American Flyer electric train. It was beautiful, a passenger train with lighted cars. I could see into the dining car where figures sat at tables. I lobbied hard for that train.

The Ancient Orchard

"Please! Please!"

I halfway expected to see it under the Christmas tree. But nobody could afford it, and anyway, we didn't have electricity. What I did get was one of the great treasures of my childhood, a Radio Flyer scooter.

As the winter progressed, we pulled planks out of the fallen barn and put down runways over the mud so we could walk to the trailer and other important places. I laid more boards beside the driveway for my Radio Flyer scooter. I coasted the length of the driveway to the paved county road and kept on going to the main highway in the valley below, then pushed the scooter back home and did it all over again. The driveway was pure mud all winter with deep ruts from end to end. It passed a couple of outbuildings and the fallen barn as it sloped down to the county road.

Mavis and Paul in the apple orchard

To get a car up the driveway meant speeding up the hill, entering the driveway fast, then gunning the engine the rest of the way to the house. Dad used to take his hands off the steering wheel and let the ruts steer the car.

When Grandpa Was a Kid

Springtime decorated the old farm with blankets of apple blossoms. Warmer weather caused our guests to hitch up their trailer and head back to Minnesota. With longer, drier days there were other things for us to do.

For instance, there was a good market for moss. Florists needed it and a forest products buyer in Centralia would buy all we could pick.

So on a dry, overcast Saturday, Dad got the family together to pick the moss that hung from the tree branches in the forest behind the farm. We each had a burlap sack which soon became full, even mine. On the way back we had to climb a steep forested hill above a creek. On the way up, I stepped on a ground hornet nest. The attack was swift. I was stung anywhere skin was exposed. I fell to the ground and tumbled out of control down the hill between the trees and brush and landed in the creek. By the time I hit the water the hornets were gone, but now I had to climb the hill again - this time in pain and dragging a heavy sack of wet moss. The moss would provide important income for our impoverished family.

Before long, green grass covered the ground and the driveway began to dry. On a walk home from school the forest invited exploration. Everything was new, and fresh with blossoms and leaves. I found snow white, three-petaled trillium growing through the forest duff. I picked some and took them home. I was told that I was not supposed pick them because the trillium plant will die when the blossom is picked.

Elsewhere in the forest, a couple of kids from a

The Ancient Orchard

neighboring farm led me to an abandoned one-room schoolhouse, which the forest was reclaiming. But, the inside of the school looked like the students and their teacher had just vanished one day and left everything behind. Papers and books were scattered about the room and the teacher's desk stood at the head of short rows of wooden desks. Everything was old.

At home, Dad found an old wagon wheel on a long wooden axle. He buried the axle straight down in the ground, leaving a wooden spoke wheel for a merry-go-round -- a nice tall one. It spun fast and easy. But the only way I could propel it was to run and jump on like a cowboy running to mount his horse. The faster I ran the faster I spun unless I failed to get a grip. Then, it was the farther I flew. About the same time, I pulled a buggy, missing almost everything but wheels, from the ruins of an outbuilding. I sat on the frame and coasted it the length of the driveway. It automatically steered in the ruts all the way from the house, to the county road where it bumped to a stop. Coasting was a joyful experience. I sang all the cowboy songs I knew as the buggy jostled along the ruts. "Let me ride to the ridge where the west commences. Gaze at the moon until I lose my senses. Don't fence me in," I sang.

On another day I stood next to a post on the porch, to watch Dad instruct Mavis in the art of shooting straight. He had his .22 rifle aimed at wooden matches sticking out of the trunk of an apple tree about 30 feet down the driveway. He fired and a match lit. He handed the rifle to Mavis and she tried. Only Dad could light matches.

Dad was good with guns. He liked every kind, and also enjoyed telling gun stories. Like when as a boy of nine, he said his father came home from Duluth with what looked like a small shotgun and a box of shells. It was a gift for my dad. Dad said he went out to the north forty, stretched out on his stomach, took aim at a woodchuck hole, and waited. After awhile, a woodchuck showed his head and dad squeezed the trigger. The blast peeled Dad off the ground and left him lying on his back. The small shotgun turned out to be an elephant rifle. My favorite gun story was the one where he made a .22 caliber machine gun out of an old alarm clock, and a single shot rifle.

When summer came, we went swimming in the Chehalis River. That river nearly took Mavis' life. She couldn't swim but somehow made it to a raft in the middle of the river, only to get shoved off by a playful boy. She sank to the bottom. On shore, Dad noticed she was gone and yelled for the boys on the raft to pull her out. They did.

Mavis, Dad and Paul with Mavis' bike on the Walters farm.

On another day, Dad took us to an auction and bought Mavis a bicycle that she would one

The Ancient Orchard

day teach me to ride.

One night when Mavis and I were home alone a black bear came up to the garbage pile, then got interested in the house and started looking in the windows. Mavis blew out the lamps and stood guard with Dad's .22 rifle. The bear didn't leave until dawn. I don't know how much else my sister did for me that year, but it must have been considerable. Too old to be a contentious sister and too young to act like a mom, she was my big sister.

We went on sightseeing drives in the big old Buick to places like Onalaska, Kelso and Mossyrock, and we went to movies. Winlock had its own little theater where our family went to a Disney movie called, *Melody Time*. In it was a short subject called, "Johnny Appleseed." Dennis Day sang a song with the words, "The Lord is good to me, and so I thank the lord for giving me the things I need, the sun, the rain and the apple seed. The Lord is good to me." This song stuck in my head permanently. I began to think of myself as blessed by God for my wonderful home in a grove of apple trees. We also went to a much more serious movie about the atomic bombs that ended World War II. The last words of the movie were, "Is this the beginning or the end?" Not a good question to put in a boy's mind. But, Winlock didn't seem much like Hiroshima. Later that question became hauntingly serious when kids were taught to dive into ditches behind the school to practice surviving an A-bomb attack.

At some point, Mom and Dad grew apart and

agreed to separate. Unknown to me, they embraced and said good-bye. Dad couldn't support his family and Mom couldn't support us all alone. The family was broken. I would stay with Dad again next summer on a different borrowed farm.

Chapter 7

Sunnydale

I moved in with Mom at the old hotel in Chehalis, where she lived. Mom worked days. This left me free to roam around town. I was given a little money for treats, which I used to buy marshmallows, cookies and pop. Sometimes I would buy matchbooks and sell them in the park for twice what I paid for them. I earned enough money to buy a balsa wood glider to fly around the park.

One day I decided to walk down to the railroad tracks. There was a small switching yard with a narrow switching tower. A head popped out of a tower window and a young man called to me, "What are you looking for?"

"I came to see the trains,"

"Come on up, I'll show you," he said. I climbed the narrow stairs to the door at the top of the tower. Inside was a small area with windows all around and a big map of the yard with switches and lights. We could see the whole yard. Cars were lined up on a siding and a switch engine was busy moving other cars around. He told me it was his job to open and close the switches so that trains could change tracks.

I told him about my rail trip west and how I thought trains were exciting. Then he warned me about the danger of trains.

"Trains can kill you," he said. "You see those switches in the yard down there. If your foot got stuck in one you couldn't get loose. You'd be run down." He opened and closed one so I could see the danger. "And never walk on railroads," he warned. "Trains go faster than they look and can come right up to you before you ever hear them, and never, ever walk on a trestle."

We talked some more about trains, then I went home.

As if on cue, Mom took me to a movie in Chehalis in which some guy ran across a dark switching yard. Sure enough, his foot got stuck in a switch, and then came the headlight of a freight train. It was just like I was told. He couldn't get his foot free and was run over by the train.

That fall I enrolled in school in Chehalis, but it wasn't long before we moved to some other little town. (It might have been Napavine) and I enrolled in a school there. Then we moved back to Chehalis. These moves had to do with Mom's need to stay employed as a waitress.

Mom took a job in a small cafe in Centralia, but soon got sick and couldn't continue with her job. Recurring infections had plagued her ever since she was a girl and was seriously ill with the 1918 swine flu, the same flu that killed my uncle Alan.

Mom told me about her stepfather, "Oscar refused to call a doctor. But when one of his horses got sick, a veterinarian was called. A horse was worth money, I wasn't."

Through good luck, or divine providence, one of her regular customers needed a caretaker for his house.

Sunnydale

Worried about leaving his place unoccupied while working out of town, he offered Mom the use of his home. All she had to do was keep an eye on it.

We moved to Sunnydale, Washington in the fall of 1947. The house was on 156th street behind Highline High School. It sat back from the road next to a long dirt driveway that continued to the back of the property. The rooms were all small, but it was sturdy and warm with three bedrooms, a kitchen and a living room. Wooden stairs went down to a sand floored cellar where home canned vegetables, fruits, and meats filled the shelves that lined one wall. We were to help ourselves to anything we wanted.

In my room there was plenty of floor space to play with my few belongings. There was also a floor model radio to listen to while I played. It had a giant speaker that wiggled the windows when I turned up the volume. My favorite show was The Lone Ranger. I had ordered a wide map of a western town, using Cheerios box tops. It showed locations for the Lone Ranger's hideout, the road where stage coaches were held up, the sheriff's office, a saloon and other important locations. I studied the map as I listened. This monstrous radio became my evening companion.

Other nights, I would lie on Mom's soft pink chenille bedspread and listen to her read from Tom Sawyer. When that book was finished she read Huckleberry Finn.

Mavis was back with us now, after living with a friend in Des Moines a few miles away. She was doing well at Highline High School, and loved being on the staff of the school newspaper.

The owner of our house was a tall handsome man with a broad smile, named Bill Montgomery. His brother, Robert Montgomery was well known to movie goers as was Robert's wife Dinah Shore. Bill worked as a sprinkler fitter. He smiled with pride when he talked of the many buildings that he "sprinkled", as he called it, and the places where he installed fire protection systems. Hard work made him prosper at everything he did. Our snug little house was his creation. So was the canned food in the cellar. At the end of the driveway he was building a large log house with trees he felled on his little piece of land. He kept hunting dogs, and raised pigs and chickens. Bill often showed up on weekends, to work on his log house. He liked to come in and drink coffee with Mom and Mavis.

At my new school I watched boys play baseball. I wanted to play, but I didn't know how, and since I was new and bashful, no one invited me to play. When the bell rang to return to class, the ball players trudged back upstairs together, and lined up at the water fountain. Although I wasn't thirsty, I lined up with them just so I could act like them. I fit in a little better in the classroom where we learned how to use pens and were trusted with our own bottle of ink. We studied local Indian people and did projects with Indian themes. This included an all day trip to the museum in Tacoma where we saw a real covered wagon. We also had art, which I loved and excelled in. But one student, Paul Boynton, outshined us all. Paul also played baseball.

Sunnydale

That fall, the principal scheduled a CO2 powered race event in the gymnasium. The racers were little cars designed to hook onto a line stretched tight just above the polished wooden floor. The escaping gas of a punctured CO2 cartridge powered the cars. I walked to a hobby shop in Burien where I bought a car kit, CO2 cartridges, glue and paint. I sat in front of the radio and built my racer.

The day of the race we had our cars on our desks. Paul Boynton's car looked professionally made. I figured his Dad helped him make it. My car failed to qualify, and was out of the race. Boynton's car probably won.

I wasn't just the new kid in school, I was gullible. I would do anything to make a friend. So when a kid in my class took me into his confidence I was ready for anything. He was going to run away from home and asked me to go with him. He lived on a little farm just kitty-corner from the school. The plan was to go to his place after school. He would go in his house and get some supplies while I waited for him in the barn. That night after school, I stood inside the barn door with a clear view of the house and waited. I could see the other boy through the kitchen window, but he didn't come back out. It got dark and still I waited. I saw his family sit down to eat. When they finished eating, his mom cleaned up the kitchen, but he still didn't come out.

I was shivering cold and dejected when I gave up waiting and headed home. It was about eight o'clock when Mom met me at the driveway.

"Were have you been?" she demanded, grabbing my shoulders.

I could hardly see her in the dark. I couldn't think of an excuse. I just hung my head.

"I've never been so worried. Go to the house," she ordered.

In the house, my mother pulled me over her lap and gave me a spanking. It was the only one she ever gave me.

"I hate doing this, but I have to." she said.

The spanking had only just begun when she stopped.

"Don't go anywhere, the sheriff's at the gate. I have to tell him we found you."

When she got back she said, "Don't you ever, ever, do that again!"

The next day I confronted the kid who abandoned me. "How come you didn't come out?" I asked.

"I forgot," was his cruel answer.

He and his friends had a good laugh at my expense.

I was getting older and wiser. *Next time someone tries to fool me I'll be ready*, I decided.

It wasn't long before some neighbor kids started picking on me. One evening, just after dark, we were playing in the street when someone started teasing me. When the taunting escalated into bullying, I gave all of them a piece of my mind, hoping to put a stop to kids laughing at my expense. I wasn't going to fall for any more tricks. Two of them grabbed me and shoved me into a sandy ditch. While some kids sat on me, others

Sunnydale

shoved sand down my neck and into my mouth and ears. I didn't stop spitting and swearing until I got home. Mom was consoling, but I don't think she said anything to the neighbors. I felt very much like a reject as I sat against the big radio in my room. It was clean and warm, and there were friendlier voices to listen to.

One Saturday, Bill, the owner of our house, took me with him to check on a job he was doing in a pier on Elliott Bay in Seattle. The vast building was filled with scaffolding going up to the massive wooden beam rafters where his company was hanging overhead piping. We were alone in the building. Every move we made echoed against the bare walls. A large door was open to the grey sky and grey water of Puget Sound. It was just as chilly and damp inside as it was outside. The air smelled of old wood and creosote.

He gave me a little education about how sprinkler systems worked, then climbed up the outside of a tall scaffold like an orangutan in bib overalls. He walked along planks laid on top of the scaffolding, checking pipes and fittings. I got the idea he was looking for leaks. On the way home he treated me to lunch at a restaurant.

On another Saturday, he was working on his log house when he came running in and grabbed a shotgun. He ran back out and blasted a blue heron right out of the sky. He took it to a taxidermist and had it stuffed.

There was a special weekend when he invited his friends and coworkers over for a feast. Bill spent all day Saturday preparing for it. He set up a large roaster under a carport-like cover next to the house. Then he killed and gutted a small pig. That evening the pig was stretched out over a grill of hot coals with a great lid covering it. All through the chill of night, Bill watched over his slow cooking pig. He catnapped and sipped beer outside my bedroom window. On Sunday, guests arrived and filled the outside tables with food and drink. I hoped Bill's actor brother, George Montgomery and his wife Dinah Shore, would show up but they didn't come. When it was time to eat, Bill uncovered his delicacy. With a little help he moved it to a long table. There lay the pig, roasted brown with a baked apple in its mouth. The air was filled with the rich aroma of roast pork. Guests ate and drank all day. So did I. There was a tub full of iced pop.

When Christmas came, Mom took me to Seattle to look at the windows and lights like she did two years before. The crowds were so thick I had to elbow my way to the windows to see the animated displays and watch electric trains coursing through snowy mountainsides.

Fredrick and Nelson was the best department store in town. A tall, slim Santa Claus in a red suit and black top hat, and no beard, greeted us. What a phony. All the real Santas were fat with white beards hooked over their ears. We rode escalators to the floor were the Christmas stuff was displayed. The whole floor was filled with every kind of decoration, wrapping, gifts, cards and more stuff than I had ever seen. From it all, Mom chose a box of bubble lights for our tree.

Sunnydale

After a movie and dinner we rode the bus home through the wet night.

Mom strung the lights across the limbs of our Christmas tree. When they were lit, bubbles glowed red, blue, green, orange and yellow. Gifts were tucked under the branches. It was Christmas Eve. Bill came over. The grownups sat in the kitchen talking and laughing while I played in the light of the tree.

"We have any pop?" I asked.

"Sorry," Mom said.

"How about a beer?" Bill joked.

"Sure," I said.

Bill sat a stubby on the floor next me. I took a sip. *Bad stuff.* The more I sipped the worse it got. About half way through I sat in the middle of floor feeling dizzy and wondering what was wrong with me.

Later, Bill slid a green wooden box under the tree. It had a lock hanging from a hasp.

"Here's the key," he said.

I unlocked it and opened the hinged lid. Inside were saws, a hammer, a drill, a block plane, screwdrivers, and enough other tools to complete a carpenter's toolbox, right down to nails and screws -- the perfect gift.

On a bright Saturday morning after Christmas, Mom and Mavis played a trick on me. I was called to the breakfast table and told I would have an ostrich egg for breakfast.

"That's an ostrich egg?" I asked.

It was huge and poached to almost done with slimy uncooked egg mucus on top. I never liked

Mom's eggs, and I sure didn't like the looks of this one. A big yellow uncooked yolk looked up at me. It filled a cereal bowl.

"I fixed it just for you," Mom said.

I looked at Mavis for reassurance.

"I had mine already," she said.

"Try it," Mom said.

"It's very good," Mavis lied.

"No thanks," I backed away.

"Just a taste," Mom coaxed.

I stuck a spoon in the partially cooked egg white, and brought a little to my mouth. It tasted sweet and sour, nothing like any egg I had tasted before.

"You can't tell anything from such a small taste," Mom said.

So I took a bigger taste. Then I recognized my ostrich egg for what it was. A half peach on top of a bowl of smoothed cottage cheese. I ate it all while Mom and Mavis had a good laugh.

Across the Des Moines Memorial Drive from my school was a small county grocery. One night Mom handed me a grocery list, a shopping bag and a flashlight.

"I need a few things from the store," she said.

It was not only dark, it was foggy. I stuck to the edge of the road and followed my beam of light. At the store I got everything Mom wanted, including a box of Pep cereal. On the backs of the boxes were cardboard trains that could be cut out and folded into railroad cars, locomotives, tenders and so on. I paid for the groceries and stuck them in the shopping bag and went out into the dark.

On the way home, I took a shortcut through the school ground. The school lights soon disappeared in the fog behind me. All I could see was a round white glow from the flashlight. I walked toward the corner of the field where a short trail led to my street. After walking for a long time, I remembered a Sergeant Preston radio show, where the Northwest Mounted Police got their man, because he walked in a circle during a blizzard. I continued on walking as straight as I could. Still I didn't reach the edge of the field. The flashlight was growing dim, and the dark fog was closing in around my feet. I was very alone and getting worried. I just couldn't reach the edge of the field. Finally I saw an earthen slope in my little circle of light, and followed it. But when I reached the corner, it was the wrong corner. With what little light was left, I turned back and followed the bank to the other corner of the field, finally reaching the trail to my street.

"What took you so long?" Mom Asked.

"I got lost."

"How can you get lost walking to the store and back?"

Spring came to Sunnydale with sun breaks between the clouds and rain. One day, in our puddled drive way, Mavis taught me to ride her bicycle. It was the one Dad had picked up at the Winlock auction. It was a full sized boy's bike and the bar was too high for me, so Mavis held the bike while I climbed on. I could just barely reach the pedals, so she pushed and ran beside me until I was on my own. The bike wobbled and I peddled. When I reached the end of the driveway, I turned right toward my school. Bike riding turned out to be a transfer skill. It balanced the same as my scooter. When I reached The Des Moines Memorial Drive, I turned right and kept on peddling past my school. After a quarter of a mile I came to 160th Avenue, where I turned right again. As the grade increased, I peddled as hard as I could. I was afraid to stop, because I couldn't get back on. After another half mile, I got to First Avenue South. Cars were on the road, so I just turned right on the dirt next to it and kept on peddling. I made a big loop back to my street. I was exhilarated and panting for air when I turned into our driveway and saw Mom and Mavis waiting for me. I coasted to a stop, the bike fell over and I was off.

"What happened to you?" Mom asked, "We were so worried."

"Why didn't you come back?" Mavis asked.

"I couldn't stop and I couldn't turn around, so I just kept turning right until I came back home."

After awhile, Mom learned that Bill's motives in offering us his home included a proposal of marriage. Bill was several years older than Mom and she wasn't interested. This caused Mom to give up her caretaking job and look for a new place to live.

As soon as summer came, Mom sent me to stay with my dad.

Chapter 8

The Little Farm in the Forest

No more third grade, no more teachers, no more nuthin'. It was summer and I was going to see my dad. Mom put me on the train in Kent and let me go alone. I sat gazing out the window for the trip from Kent, south to Centralia. It reminded me of three years earlier when Mom, Mavis and I took the train from Duluth to Seattle to join Dad. The train was exciting. A real steam locomotive was pulling me along!

A steam locomotive is a living machine. Heavy with iron, coal, water and fire, it rumbles across steel rails nailed to wooden ties on a bed of gravel. Black cinder-filled smoke pours from its stack, and white steam bursts from its cylinders, driving lattices of huge steel rods across giant steel wheels. The steam whistle cries and howls and hot oil drips onto the squirming road below, while the fireman shovels coal into the hungry mouth of the red-hot firebox and the engineer pulls levers, driving the engine forward.

From where I sat I could hear the steady click and clack of the wheels crossing the rail joints, as the lush green of the Puget Sound lowlands passed outside the window. Sometimes a bit of smoke from the engine would drift into view.

The train came to a slow stop at the little Centralia station. From my window, I saw Dad standing on the sunlit platform wearing a plaid shirt and a big smile.

Dad's old Buick limousine was now a pickup

truck. He had cut off everything behind the front seat and boarded it in. He added a wooden flat bed on the back. We got in and started off through Centralia and Chehalis toward Winlock. On the way I told him all about what I did over the winter. How Mom read me *Tom Sawyer* while she was sick, and that my room had a big radio where I listened to the *Lone Ranger* and the *Green Hornet*. I told him how fun it was to turn out the light and sit with my back against the radio, so I could feel the vibrations and become scared listening to *The Shadow* that started with the announcer saying, "Who knows what evil lurks in the hearts of man? The shadow knows."

I told him, "I learned to ride Mavis' bicycle and she gave it to me."

"I did some logging," Dad said. Then he said, "How do you like the way I turned the Buick into a pickup?"

I remembered the big back seat and the fun rides I had in it, the tubs of water that we carefully took home from the dump and the time we outran the sheriff. "It's okay," I answered.

"I'm glad I did it," he went on. "A logger I was working with got hurt bad. We had no way to get him out of the woods except on the back of my pickup. A couple of my buddies watched over him while I drove him to the hospital in Centralia."

The roads narrowed as we got closer to my dad's borrowed house. Eventually the pavement ended and we continued on a gravel road, then up a long sloping hill through the forest, past the forty acres we once

The Little Farm in the Forest

owned. At the end of the road we turned onto a dusty driveway and continued past a pond, a small field of oats and a big old barn. We stopped in front of a weathered cabin with one window and a door in front.

There by a small covered porch, stood my Radio Flyer scooter. Inside was a room with a single bed and a couch. A clarinet hung from a set of deer antlers mounted on the wall and Dad's violin lay on a small table. The kitchen was tiny and stuck out from the back of the cabin like a wart. It had a small iron cook stove, a little table for two, and almost no cupboards. All this belonged to Dave Knokes, the dairy farmer who lived a half-mile down the dirt road, across from what was our forty-acre forest. This would be my home with Dad for the next few weeks.

My bed that night was the couch. Our only light came from a half pound coffee can full of bacon grease, with some kind of wick in it. It made black smoke while providing minimum illumination. When I went to bed, Dad played some sentimental tunes on his violin. His giant black shadow moved about the room as he played. Later, Dad propped himself up next to the makeshift lamp and opened a book.

As it got late, I got homesick. After a while, Dad came and sat with me. "You'll be okay." He then told comforting stories until I fell asleep to his soft voice, and the pleasant aroma of bacon grease and cigarette smoke.

Morning was bacon and eggs with biscuits.

"I don't like fried eggs," I said.

"Let's see if I can cook them so you like them,"

When Grandpa Was a Kid

He sliced thick strips of bacon and laid them in a black iron frying pan, and then popped biscuits into the oven. I sat and watched the yellow flames around the stove lids and smelled the biscuits, bacon and wood smoke as the room warmed. Out came the bacon and in went the eggs. The eggs cooked on both sides at the same time, as Dad splashed bacon fat over the eggs with his spatula. Then everything was ready. Warm butter melted into the hot biscuits and the eggs were delicious. Dad knew how to cook.

Dad assigned me the task of fetching water from the small pond down at the end of the driveway past the barn and oat field. The water came fresh from the earth through a pipe driven horizontally into the bank that rose above the pond. Dragonflies, large and small, colored like neon tubes hovered and darted above the water. On the surface were insects that walked on water and in the pond were other insects and polliwogs. This was a place of great wonder. It took me a long time to return with a pail of water.

Dave Knokes had a granddaughter my age. It was she who had lit the fire in our forty-acre forest, two years earlier. One day she came with her grandpa Dave and his brother-in-law. The two farmers went right to work, leaving us kids free to play. Like farm kids everywhere, we climbed to the top of the ladder in the barn and dove into the hay until we were tired, then sat by the pond until her grandpa took her home.

Sometimes Dad let me visit her by myself. Since she lived at the bottom of the hill, I coasted my scooter all the way to her farm. Halfway down the hill was the

The Little Farm in the Forest

rotting carcass of a horse that lay beside the road. It looked like it had just tipped over into the ditch while it was going about its usual business. Its nose was buried in soft grass with its mouth open almost like it was about to take a bite. Long teeth and large hoofs told me it was an old work horse. Its life just ended one day and there it was dead in the ditch. A haze of flies buzzed around its bloated body and maggots crawled in its flesh. By summer's end there would be just a few bones hidden in the tall grass and the old work horse would be forgotten about.

Dad avoided regular work, although he had done a little logging. Now he lived from hand to mouth gathering forest products, picking fruit and hunting. He seemed to enjoy the lifestyle.

He needed some money so Dad grabbed an empty gunny sack and off we walked into the forest next to the farm in search of moss. Moss demanded a high price from florists. After a while we found moss hanging from old tree limbs. Dad pulled it off the limbs with a little help from me. When his bag was stuffed, we started back toward the farm. The trail led us past a small pond. Right there by the water, Dad fell to the ground. He lay still with his .22 rifle beside him and the big bag of moss by his shoulder. I could see Dad was breathing but why was he just lying on the ground?

"Dad, Dad!" He didn't move. "Oh God," I prayed. "Please don't let my daddy die."

Douglas fir trees stood tall above the undergrowth, and closed the forest from the sun. I began to imagine dangers that I couldn't see. I picked up Dad's rifle and waited. I was especially afraid of cougars. I stood there. The forest was so huge and I was so alone. Finally he sat up. Then he stood and we continued to walk back to the cabin.

"I'm sorry." he said. "Sometimes I get dizzy, but I rarely pass out."

I carried the rifle and we talked the rest of the way home. He looked so tired.

The next day we again went looking for forest products. This time it was sword ferns. They had to be just the right length, measured from the fingertips to the armpit. Dad cut them with a sharp little finger hook and bound them fifty-two ferns to a bundle. By the end of the day he had a lot of bundles. The next morning after another bacon, egg and biscuit breakfast, we loaded them on the back of the Buick along with the bag of moss we picked earlier, and left for the Centralia forest products dealer to sell them. On the way, we stopped at a gas station. It was already becoming a hot day.

"Here's a dime, go get a cold bottle of pop," he said.

I pulled open the screen door and went inside. The pop bottles stood in a large metal pop cooler, up to their necks in icy water. There were dozens of them to sort through; Bierlies, Nehi, Quench, Pepsi, and every other kind. I settled on a Dad's Root Beer. I stuck it in the bottle opener and pried off the cap, threw my dime on the counter and went back outside, squinting my eyes in the late morning sun. The attendant was

The Little Farm in the Forest

gassing up the Buick. I took a long cold drink of root beer and went to stand next to Dad.

Army surplus Studebaker trucks converted to log trucks, were going by loaded with huge logs.

"There goes the last of the virgin timber around here," Dad said. He pointed toward the Cascade Mountains in the distance. "Soon it will all be gone."

Then he handed me a box of firecrackers he bought in the gas station, big red ones that looked like little sticks of dynamite.

In Centralia, we sold the forest products and continued north to pick strawberries. We drove past Tumwater and the big Olympia brewery, to the Yelm highway and then on to Pattison Lake. It was late in the day when we arrived. A dirt road went straight between two strawberry fields to a lakeside park. There were rows of cabins for fruit pickers to live in. We were given one. These were no ordinary cabins. They were made from large wooden crates about eight feet square. They were left over packing crates from World War II, which had been trucked in from the Bremerton shipyards and placed in rows. Each crate had a board door on the front and wooden bunk bed pallets on the back wall to sleep on. There were two outhouses and a communal water faucet to round out our accommodations. Over near the lake was a tiny snack bar that sold Green River drinks. Dad let me buy one. There were lots of kids who made friends quickly. Some had dark skin and were called Mexicans. There were some gypsy kids too. I joined them and we played kick the can until after dark.

When Grandpa Was a Kid

Early the next morning, I dug into my box of firecrackers and walked down to the lake. Everything was still and the lake was smooth. I lay prone on the dock looking down into the clear water. After a while some trout started nibbling at the pilings. I carefully reached into my pocket for a firecracker, and lit it. It dropped quietly from my hand into the lake. It sank with the fuse sizzling in the water. The explosion was a large silver sphere that immediately burst to the surface with a loud blast. The echo came back from across the lake. The explosion startled me. I quickly returned to our cabin afraid I would be in some kind of trouble, but no one seemed to notice.

We picked strawberries all day. Dad squatted over the plants, picking fast. I followed along on my hands and knees, picking slow. It seemed like everything took forever. Eventually, a flat was filled with strawberries and we could get up and walk to where the farmer collected them. He marked down what we picked and then we went back and started all over again. The process seemed to go on forever until it was finally lunch time which was nothing more than some bread and cheese. Afternoon seemed even longer. But finally, when the day was done and dinner was eaten, I had plenty of energy to play kick the can till sun down.

I didn't pick very many strawberries, but I sure ate a lot. On the third day I began to itch. My skin broke out in hives. Dad knew the cure. He checked us out and we drove home. Back on the farm he fed me whiskey jiggers full of Milk of Magnesia and ordered

The Little Farm in the Forest

me to sit in the outhouse. The next day the hives, and everything in me, were gone.

Late one night, I was gently awakened. "Shhh! be absolutely quiet. There's a deer on the porch," Dad whispered.

The only light was from the stars through the window. I could barely see Dad level his rifle. He fired right through the door. I heard the deer collapse on the porch. Dad went outside to hang it and gut it. As I slept, Dad butchered and canned the venison. When I woke up he was in the kitchen processing the last jars. For the rest of my visit, we ate tender cold venison right from the jars.

Dad claimed not to like cats, but he would sit with one on his lap and pet it while he read. He also thought it was his duty to kill extra cats. There was an extra cat on the farm. Dad decided to include me in the execution of this unlucky animal. He had me hold the cat by the scruff its neck, while he leveled his .22 rifle at the cat's head.

"Be very still," he cautioned.

Just as he squeezed the trigger, I let go of the cat. The bullet just grazed it. With a loud shriek, it dashed into the oat field. I never saw it again.

Winlock held its annual egg festival. After all, they thought they were the egg capital of the world. A carnival came to town, picnic tables were set up, and plenty of people showed up to have a good time. The highlight of the festival -- as anyone could guess -- was fried eggs. A huge frying pan, about eight feet across, was placed over a wide fire near the giant golden egg town symbol. The pan was greased with slabs of bacon. Cooks stood around cracking and flipping eggs. After a lunch of eggs Dad bought me a hydrogen-filled balloon to carry around. On the way home it touched Dad's cigarette and blew up, scorching the Buick's headliner, as well as our hair.

One morning Dave Knokes and his brother-in-law were already at work in the barn while Dad and I were eating breakfast.

Suddenly Dave's brother-in-law burst through the door yelling, "Dave's a dyin', Dave's a dyin' "

Dad shot out of the house with me behind him. There was Dave lying on his back in the barnyard hemorrhaging from his mouth. I stood horrified. Dad found a towel and started removing clots of blood from Dave's mouth.

Dad looked right at me and said, "Get to a phone".

I grabbed my scooter and started down the driveway as fast as gravity and my kicking foot would allow. As I neared the horse carcass, I saw Dave's pickup coming with the brother-in-law at the wheel and Dad bent over Dave in the back. They quickly vanished in a cloud of dust. I realized that my rush to the phone was intended to spare me from watching Dave die. I slowed down and looked at the old work horse where it fell and began to cry.

Dave died from tuberculosis. I was present at the railhead when his casket was crated for its trip to Sacramento, California, where he grew up. We stood and watched the nails being driven in the crate that held his coffin. Then watched as it was carefully placed in a rail car and the door shut behind it. Three days later Dave's wife died. After that, I was sent back home to Kent. It would be a long time before I saw my Dad again.

When Grandpa Was a Kid

Chapter 9

Seven Gables

Mom met me at the train station in Kent where she and Mavis had moved while I was gone. Our new home was just a short walk from the station. It was a small upstairs apartment in a large old house on Gowe Street. Mavis took a job tying flies for Shoff's sporting goods store on Meeker Street in front of our apartment. Mom worked a block farther west on Meeker Street, at a family owned restaurant. Since I had returned from my visit with Dad earlier than expected, I found myself unsupervised while Mom and Mavis worked.

For a town of one square mile there was plenty to see, and I couldn't wait to explore it. Kent was the hub for the surrounding farm economy. During the week, trucks carried farm produce and milk to the processing plants, and trucks and trains hauled processed foods out of town. The farm produce factories were busy preparing strawberry jam, canned beans, rhubarb, raspberries, cherries, and much more. One processor made sauerkraut. When the lids on the fermenting vats were opened, the whole town stunk.

Kraft Foods had a dairy processing plant that let me take a tour. The canned milk didn't smell too good, but they sent me on my way with a small glass of bacon/cheddar cheese spread that I ate with my fingers while I walked the busy streets. On Saturday, Meeker Street was bumper-to-bumper traffic as families came to town for shopping. On Sunday everything was

When Grandpa Was a Kid

closed while the town rested in near silence.

Trains were easy to hear from anywhere in town. I couldn't resist the pull of these great machines. I sometimes stood close enough to the tracks to feel the ground shake and the wind suck at me, as they sped through town. Freight trains, with as many as one hundred cars, moved more slowly, backing up traffic. Some trains stopped and started. The big steam locomotives could spin their wheels on the tracks with a powerful burst of steam, like skates sparking on ice.

One warm sunny day, I decided to walk along the railroad tracks. I left town heading south. I walked just above raspberry fields and truck farms, always on the lookout for trains. When I saw one approach, I stepped away from the tracks and watched it go by. Before long I came to a trestle that had two sets of tracks, about ten feet above some water. I had been warned never to cross a railroad bridge, but since the railroad had two sets of tracks, I reasoned that if a train came while I was crossing, I could continue on the unused track. But what if there was a train on both tracks? Then I would have to jump off. But I couldn't swim. Maybe I could hang from the end of a tie. Then I noticed that halfway across, the railroad ties extended far enough out to hold a barrel; a safe haven if I could only make it halfway across. I looked both ways down the tracks until they converged and disappeared in the distance. No trains. I stepped onto the trestle and began to cross, being careful of where I stepped. I looked up and down the tracks, still no trains.

When I reached the middle of the trestle I paused

at the barrel, checked again for trains, then continued across the second half. As I neared the end of the trestle, I looked back once again, but this time there was a train in the distance. I quickened my pace, but every footstep had to land on a tie or I would fall. I glanced over my shoulder and saw the train getting bigger. I no longer watched the train, I just ran till I was clear of the bridge. I stepped away from the railroad track and waited for the train to pass. The train didn't make a sound until it was on the trestle, then I felt the tremble and saw circles of water rippling out from the pilings below. As quickly as the train was in front of me, it was gone.

My walk in the country-scared the heck out of me. I wanted off the tracks, but home was back across the trestle. This time, after looking again for trains, I just walked across as quickly as I could and kept going until I reached Kent. Years later, two children were killed crossing that bridge

In my travels about town I met other unsupervised kids. We ran all over town, to the movies, into the second hand stores and to the dime store for glasses of Coke.

That fall, I enrolled in school a few blocks away. I remember nothing about school, but after school I had a routine. First, I would look for a casserole or other food that Mom had waiting for me. Then I listened to radio shows programmed especially for kids who just got home from school. At four o'clock, Bobby Benson and the B-Bar-B Riders, came on. At four-thirty it was Sergeant Preston of the Yukon.

Later that fall, Mom changed jobs. We moved to a tiny house on highway 99 that Mom shared with another waitress. They both worked at the Seven Gables Restaurant next door

The Seven Gables was a large restaurant with a horseshoe counter in front and booths and a dance floor behind. The owner, Leo Hassan, and his family lived upstairs. He was the cousin of Alex Jabor who owned the Happy Haven restaurant in Bow Lake (SeaTac) three miles north.

One of Mom's regular customers was a tall man with reddish blond hair, who looked like Charles Lindberg. There were lots of regular customers, but this one came in to see Mom.

Virgil always wore brown pants with his army belt and shiny buckle. He worked as a welder and sometimes wore his little black asbestos welder's cap. He and Mom soon became close friends. Then one night, he came to the house to take Mom some place.

"Hi Paul", he said in a serious tone of voice.

"Hi," I said.

"How's school?" he asked.

"Fine, I'm going to the same school I went to in the first grade."

"What grade are you in now?"

"Fourth."

"Do you play ball?" He asked.

"No."

Some kids from school played baseball behind the restaurant, but I was too timid to join in. The next day Mom told me that Virgil said I didn't seem to like him.

Seven Gables

I thought over our conversation.

"Yes I do," I said.

"He said you snubbed him."

"I did not!"

This was my first experience with Virgil's jealousy.

One Saturday afternoon, Virgil and two of his friends, Bill Thompson and Don Thomas, came to the house. Like Virgil, they were handsome men in their late thirties. But, these guys were the terrors of Highway 99. They spent evenings next door at the Seven Gables drinking beer, then sped away together on war surplus motorcycles, weaving through cars that obeyed the 60-mile-an-hour speed limit. Bill's arm and shoulder were in a cast from an alcohol-soaked driving accident. Don had recently recovered from third degree burns, which he suffered when he slopped gas on his leg while filling up his old Ford. When he got in the car, he lit a cigarette and burst into flames.

Virgil and Mom

These fun loving, foul mouthed alcoholics were still fighting the Second World War and would never get over it. They were nothing like Virgil, who was conservative in all things. But they were fellow veterans and welders who worked together.

Sometime after Bill got his cast off, I was in the

When Grandpa Was a Kid

back yard playing with some kittens and cardboard boxes, listening to the fun and laughter coming from the house, when the door opened. Mom, Virgil, Bill and Don stuck their heads out.

I heard Mom whisper, "Watch this," as she stepped out on the porch.

Then she asked, "What are you doing, Paul?"

"I'm building me a cat house," I said.

Everybody laughed and snickered.

"I could use one of those," Bill grinned.

"What do you do with your cat house?" Don asked.

"I put kittens in it." The laughter increased.

I liked these guys. They thought I was fun. Mom ushered them back in the house where the laughter continued. I returned to building my cathouse.

Paul with neighbor Wayne Hanks

That winter it snowed. It began on a Friday night. I stood alone under a yard light and watched the black night sky become a lighted cone of falling snow.

By morning, several inches covered the ground. With my mittened hands clutching my BB gun, I went bird hunting in the woods a quarter mile from home. A delicate grey and white Chickadee stood belly deep on a snowy branch. I raised my BB gun and aimed with the ease of an experienced hunter. I slowly

Seven Gables

squeezed the trigger. The bird flipped from the branch in a puff of white. In the same instant, pain shot up my arm and a cry burst from my lips. My fingers were stuck in the lever of the gun. When I was finally able to lift the lever, my fingers were red and grooved and had begun to swell. With my good hand, I stuffed my right coat pocket with snow, and painfully slid my injured hand into the pocket. I picked up my BB gun and trudged home. I walked into the Seven Gables, BB gun in hand.

"Mom," I called.

She was standing at the counter talking to Virgil.

"What's the matter?" My tone of voice had startled her.

"I got my fingers stuck in the BB gun."

I held out my hand. By now, my fingers were double their normal size.

"Oh no," Mom cried.

Virgil said he would take me to the hospital.

In the car I explained what happened. A lever action BB gun uses the lever as a pump. When the lever is pulled open it forces a strong spring into a tightly coiled position. It took all my strength to cock it. Once the lever is all the way open it locks the spring. Then the lever is closed easily into a securing clip. My clip was worn out from repeated use, allowing the lever to fall open when I raised my gun. When I pulled the trigger, the spring was released forcing air and a BB from my gun. At the same time, the spring slammed the lever against my fingers.

At the Renton General Hospital, the doctor told us

that my fingers and tendons were bruised. He placed my hand on a stiff board and wrapped it.

"Take it off in a week, it should be fine," he said.

"Why do you shoot birds anyway?" Mom wanted to know.

"Dad wants me to learn to hunt," I said. But inwardly I couldn't get the vision of the bird from my mind. I felt its pain.

When the weather warmed, a wide winter pond formed in the field behind the restaurant. I carved a three-inch long wooden ship hull and fitted it with a foremast and a mainmast, both covered with waxed paper sails. I imbedded a Gem razor blade on the bottom for ballast and a keel. By twisting the masts, I could determine its tack. I moved the masts to match the wind direction, and then set my little windjammer loose on the pond. It leaned to one side as the breeze propelled it across the little ripples of the pond, while I ran around to the other side to intercept it. I reset the masts and watched it sail back the other way.

Weekends were never boring. If I wasn't sailing on the pond, I went hunting with my repaired BB-Gun or hiked along the highway in search of matchbooks to add to my collection. But one Sunday my routine was interrupted with real adventure.

I was spending the afternoon with a pile of comic books, when I heard the whine of a diving airplane. I ran out in the yard just in time to see a red streak clear our chimney by fifty feet and shoot back up into the sky. I watched the small red airplane wheel around higher and higher above our house, and then tip forward. The whine of its engine grew louder as it came down, right at me.

"Mom! Mom!" I yelled.

Mom was already running out of the house, her hands waving in the air.

"What's the matter with him? He has no business scaring children half to death." She yelled,

The airplane almost straddled our chimney with its black puffy wheels, and flew off beyond the treetops.

"He not only drives like a maniac, he flies like one," Mom said."

"Do you know who that was?" I asked.

"It's that drunken Bill Thompson. Are you all right, Paul?"

"I'm fine."

Actually I was thrilled. I watched the sky waiting for him to do it again so I could wave at him, but he didn't come back. The rest of the day, I asked questions about Bill Thompson's airplane.

"Mom, do you think Bill would take me for a ride?" I asked.

"No!"

"Maybe he would take you for a ride and I could go along?"

"I don't think so!"

"What if he asked you to go flying, would you?"

"Maybe."

"Mom, it would be a lot of fun. Can't you at least ask?"

"Well I'll see." she said.

When Grandpa Was a Kid

The next Saturday morning, Bill Thompson's Chevy pickup pulled into the yard. He came to take us flying. His red Piper Cub was parked in the grass at the Kent Airfield. We drove up to it and stopped.

"How much do you weigh?" Bill asked me.

"I don't know."

Mom assured him that I weighed less than the 80-pound cargo limit. Since this was a two passenger plane, I would ride in the cargo compartment behind the seats. Bill got me strapped in, then started the engine. We taxied onto the grassy runway. Then with a roar we went bouncing along gaining speed until suddenly we lifted free of the ground. My heart raced with excitement, and a little fear, as we climbed above the valley. Below was a patchwork of farms in hues of greens and browns with the City of Kent planted among them. I saw cars on the West Valley Highway, and as we flew higher I saw the Milwaukee Railroad, and the twisting Green River. We turned west toward Puget Sound. Before long, we were over Des Moines. I could see the homes of two of Mavis' friends; the Marsten's little farm and Mrs. Archer's waterfront acreage beside the wide blue Puget Sound. Bill gave us a panoramic view of the coastline, and then flew back over the land.

Bill pointed down and yelled, "There's the Seven Gables!"

Suddenly the nose tipped down and we dove toward the ground. Mom yelled above the loud whine of the dive. Bill was getting a tongue-lashing. My stomach lifted into my throat, then shot down into my gut as we pulled up over the roof of our house. Once we leveled off and Mom caught her breath she turned to me and asked, "Are you alright, Paul?"

"yeah," I beamed.

Mom wasn't much of a yeller, but she managed to raise her voice above the roar of the engine to chew Bill out for his acrobatics.

Back on the ground, Bill cracked a broad smile and asked, "Well Paul, was that the ride you wanted?"

"Yes exactly. Thanks a million," I smiled

I never saw Bill's plane above our house again, but I never forgot the thrill of that little red airplane.

On April 13, 1949, I was home from school recovering from the mumps. Virgil was in the living room waiting for Mom, who was singing and dancing around in the bedroom while she got dressed.

"Vi! Stop dancing around. You're shaking the whole house," Virgil yelled.

But his face was fearful as he realized it wasn't Mom. I ran to the front window. Virgil's two-tone green 1941 Plymouth rolled up and down the driveway three feet in each direction. Everything shook. Things fell down and tipped over. It was an earthquake, which, we learned later, was of a 7.1 magnitude, and was the most violent earthquake ever recorded in Western Washington. Although it only shook for 30 seconds, eight people lost their lives, several more were injured, and many homes were destroyed. Thousands of chimneys collapsed, four schools were ruined and condemned. In Olympia, parts of the stone state office buildings lay on the ground. The capitol dome nearly collapsed. The quake was felt as far away as British Columbia, Montana and Northern California.

Mom and Virgil forgot about where they were going. Instead, they sat and talked about the earthquake. In a few minutes, Chief, an old man Mom knew, knocked on the door. He was visibly shaken.

"I was under the Spanish Castle leveling the floor when the building started shaking," he said. With wide-open eyes and shaking hands, he continued. "The Castle has no foundation, just rows of four-by-four posts. I could see daylight on top of each post as the building rocked back and forth. I was terrified. I thought I would be crushed to death. I crawled as fast as I could, but kept getting knocked over. When I finally got out, I ran to my truck and got the hell out of there."

The Spanish Castle was a large wooden dance hall, just two miles away in Midway. It looked like a tall castle sticking out of a wide gravel parking lot. Young people came from all around the area to dance away the nights to the swing bands of the time.

Our school was undamaged, but the playground was littered with rocks and stones that pushed up out of the ground during the earthquake. Many of them contained iron pyrite crystals. We kids thought we had found gold and filled our pockets. From my classroom I could see the nearly completed terminal building at SeaTac airport. I wondered if it was okay.

Before long, school returned to normal, except for a visit from the Gideon Society. Two missionaries came with stacks of pocket sized New Testaments to hand out. They told us the story of how Jesus, "God's only begotten son", died a painful death, so that our sins could be forgiven. All we had to do was believe in Jesus, then we would be saved, and go to heaven when we died. We were told another story of a soldier fighting in Korea, who was shot in the chest, but saved when the bullet lodged in his Gideon New Testament. The books were handed out. Then we were asked if we wanted to be saved. While our heads were bowed, we were led in prayer.

Then we were told, "If you prayed with us and accepted Jesus into your heart, write your name and today's date inside the back cover of your New Testament."

I wrote my name in the book. That night I went home with a New Testament in my shirt pocket -- bullet proof.

When Grandpa Was a Kid

Chapter 10

Briscoe Memorial School

In the spring of 1948, Mom moved again. This time home was a room in the basement of Alex Jabor's house in Bow Lake, an early name for the City of SeaTac. It sat directly behind the Happy Haven restaurant, which the Jabor's owned and where Mom now waited tables. I was left to do whatever I wanted. I was close enough to school that I could walk or ride my bike.

Since Mom worked so close, I would sometimes go to the Happy Haven and sit at the horseshoe bar, where I talked to customers. I learned how to get them to buy me things.

Happy Haven Restaurant on highway 99 in Bow Lake (Now SeaTac)

Above the back of the bar, where the punchboard prizes were displayed, were some giant Hershey bars. I started conning the man sitting next to me at the bar.

"That's sure a big Hershey bar," I said casually.

He looked up from his beer glass, "sure is."

"I wonder what it would be like to have one all to yourself," I said.

"You'd like to have that wouldn't you?"

"I sure would."

The man bought it for me. When Mom found out, I was banned from the bar.

My circumstances must have worried Mavis because her well-to-do friends, the Marstons, suggested a private Catholic school for me.

"Oh Paul, you'll love it there," Mom said.

"There's boating and horseback riding, and you can come home on week-ends."

I had visions of academies for privileged boys, like the ones advertised on the back pages of the National Geographic Magazine. I thought of tall brick buildings and rows of young men in uniforms. I imagined canoes slicing through blue water, and ponies on polo fields. I was ready to go.

Briscoe Memorial School sat next to the Green River, at the end of a long gravel road. It was an aged three-story brick building, just as I had imagined, neatly separated from the peaceful farmland of the Kent Valley by chain link fences.

In the school courtyard, a black robed Catholic brother welcomed us to the school. A friend of Mom's who drove us there, waited by his car smoking a cigarette. Mom and I were taken inside to a locker room. I put my few belongings on a wooden bench and sat down beside them. The brother quickly inspected everything, and handed Mom a few things that weren't allowed at Briscoe, like my matchbook collection. Then my pockets were emptied. The brother handed Mom my pocketknife.

"We don't allow knives," he said.

Even my shoes were looked at to see what might

be inside. Finally the brother put my remaining possessions into my locker. I stayed seated on the wooden bench while Mom and the brother stepped away to talk in private. When Mom returned she had some unsettling news, something about new boys staying for a while before they could visit home. *Oh well*, I thought, *just that much more to talk about when I got home*. Mom gave me a beautiful smile and a cheery, "toodle-loo", and left.

The brother led me to a classroom and introduced me to Brother McCormack, My new teacher. Both men were dressed alike in black cassocks. Brother McCormack introduced me to the class, and then made a point of telling everyone how much more advanced Briscoe boys were than public school children -- like me. He assigned me a seat, and class resumed.

At lunch we went to a cafeteria where we stood in line to fill our plates, then sat at rows of tables. No one could talk or eat before the food was prayed over. After lunch, we went to a large fenced play yard. I could see the Green River, and wondered if there were canoes there.

"Why are you here?" a boy in my room wanted to know.

"My mom can't take care of me," I said.

"Mine couldn't take care of me, either. I kept getting in trouble, so I had to come here,"

"Where are the canoes?" I asked

"Canoes? What canoes?"

Another boy said it was either here or jail for him. He told me I wouldn't like it. "It's a prison." He said.

When Grandpa Was a Kid

When recess ended, everyone ran for the door. Since everyone else ran, so did I. There was no space between us as we pushed our way through the door.

The boy next to me said. "The last one off the playground gets a whipping."

Since we were so close together, there was no last one, so there was no whipping. I figured the kid was lying. The same rush ended the afternoon recess.

Paul stood where these boys stand --- PI photo

At dinner, I was given a job helping with the dishes. Everyone had a job. The attitude of the brothers around the kitchen wasn't very kindly. But I didn't expect kindness from teachers anyway. That evening I was assigned a bed in a large dormitory. Across the room was a row of sinks and mirrors. The routine was to wash and brush your teeth, then change into pajamas. When the lights were turned out, we knelt by our beds for prayer. That night, I lay in my new bed and listened to the sounds in the room. From across the valley, I could hear the familiar sound of train whistles.

The next morning, the cafeteria had a strange odor to it. Oatmeal and dried eggs seemed to be the reason. I ate my Spartan breakfast and then helped with the dishes.

Just like Brother McCormack said, I was way behind the rest of the class. They studied more than any kids I knew, and they were good at spelling.

Briscoe Memorial School

Spelling was something I never paid much attention to, but spelling would become dangerously important at Briscoe. After a couple of days, we had a spelling quiz. Any boy who misspelled a word was called to the front of the room where Brother McCormack sat in his chair. The boy was asked to hold out his hand, palm down. Then Brother McCormick hit it hard with a leather strap, one strike for each misspelled word. I probably missed half the words. I went to the front of the room last. I stuck out my hand and waited for the strap to come down. Then, I moved my hand. Whack! The strap hit Brother McCormack's leg. He threatened me with bodily harm if I ever did that again. Again I held out my hand. Again he bore down with his strap with all of his might. Again I withdrew my hand. Again he whipped his own leg. He jumped out of his chair and grabbed my wrist. I received the rest of my strapping with his hand firmly around my wrist. All I could do was kick, yell and swear. I'm sure I didn't miss as many words as I was strapped for. I was transformed into a hateful, but dutiful speller.

Because I claimed not to be Catholic, I was excused from Catechism. I was told to stand by the window with my back to the class until Catechism was over. This was the best part of the day. I looked across the valley at farmhouses and fields and longed to be far away.

The yard was where I learned how things worked at Briscoe.

One of the boys told me, "You get a beating for any thing you do wrong. You don't want to cause trouble."

"Why?" I wanted to know.

"They want you to be afraid of them, they can do whatever they want with you, and you'll be afraid to tell." he said.

From playground conversations with classmates, I learned that some had been abused at home or had no home, and were living at Briscoe out of charity. Some were delinquents whose families were trying to keep them out of trouble.

When the bell rang one kid was off daydreaming and didn't make it to the door in time. Sure enough, He got a whipping. A leather strap snapped several times across his butt.

One night I didn't brush my teeth. Brother McCormack waited until I was undressed and ready to put on my pajamas, to remind me. He grabbed me by the ear and jerked me off my feet, dragging me like a hooked fish toward the sinks across the room.

"We brush our teeth every night, and don't you forget it," he snarled, as he shoved me up against a cold porcelain sink.

Standing naked in front of a dormitory full of curious boys, I brushed my teeth. Then suddenly he had me by the ear again, and off we went to my bed. I was sure my ear was going to rip right off my head. I was thrown to the floor where I said my prayers in a darkened room under the stare of the evil Brother McCormack. Had he heard my prayer, he would have beaten me to death, and had my prayer been answered he would have vanished in a vapor, to burn in the depths of hell. Finally, I lay crying in bed waiting to hear the train whistles from across the valley.

Bathing was a group activity. We got undressed at our desks and walked as a single naked line across the hall to a long narrow shower room. Brother McCormack ducked into a control booth with a window facing the row of showers. He had complete control of the water. He changed it from hot to cold and from cold to hot as he laughed and yelled orders. We jumped around in misery until the shower ended with ice-cold water. How could this imposter pose as a man of God? I wondered.

I felt trapped with boys no one wanted, locked away next to the Green River with their teachers and tormentors, and no canoes.

In the yard I discussed escape plans with one of my classmates.

"If I could get over the fence I would run for it," I said. "I know my way home."

"Some boys have run away but they always get caught. The school pays fifty-cents to anyone who catches a runaway. No matter how many kids catch you," he told me.

Then he told me a story about someone who didn't get caught. He pointed a finger to a dock on the river where some garbage barrels stood.

"Trusted kids get jobs emptying garbage into the river. One guy dumped the garbage, then climbed into the empty barrel and floated away down the river."

"Did he get away?" I asked.

"No! He drowned," the other boy said.

When Grandpa Was a Kid

Was I being lied to? Or was this another incredible story that would prove to be true?

I was afraid of the river and turned my attention back to the fence. Climbing it would be too slow, but if I could somehow jump over I would have a long head start, or maybe not be noticed at all. The yard had large swings that weren't fastened down. They could be dragged close to the fence where I might be able to swing high enough to bail out over the fence. I could be a mile away by the time recess ended. I went to the swings and practiced bailing out, but attracted too much attention as I repeatedly flew out of the swing several feet up only to fall straight to the ground. There had to be a way out. I thought about jumping out a window, but soon rejected that idea. I decided the best way out was to tell Mom what was going on. If she believed me, she would take me out. But, how would I do that? I didn't even know my own address and Mom had no phone.

Sunday was Mass. We sat in the little chapel and watched. There wasn't anything else to do since the service was in Latin. Some boys were up front on their knees with their mouths open eating something put on their tongues.

I asked the boy next to me, "What are they doing?"

"They're putting little pieces of Saint Peter's body in their mouths," he whispered. Then he added. "Don't get caught talking during Mass."

My birthday came. No one cared. I moped around until one of the brothers asked what was wrong.

"It's my birthday. I want to go home," I said.

That evening an older boy came for me and led me up stairs to the sympathetic brother's room. He sat at a desk with a piece of chocolate cake in front of him. He slid it across the desk to me, and said, "Happy birthday."

I cried. Somebody cared. Then suddenly I was gripped with hope. I saw a phone on his desk.

"Can I call my mom?" I asked.

"Well, we usually don't allow calls, but it is your birthday," he said.

While I ate my cake, he got through to Mom where she worked.

"Mom?"

"Happy Birthday Paul," she said.

"Mom you gotta get me out of here!" I unloaded about the leather strap and the ear pulling. She sounded worried.

The brother reached for the phone.

"I'll call you back." She said.

I went to sleep a happy boy that night.

I waited every minute for Mom to call. Then on the second or third evening after my birthday I was called to the nice brother's room. It was a call from Mom. But, she questioned me about what I told her. *Didn't she believe me?* "Please Mom you have to believe me. Please take me home." I begged.

The call ended in uncertainty.

I hung around with the nice brother for a while. He prayed for me and gave me a rosary. That was very comforting to me, but now I would be expected to join in Catechism class.

I did well at spelling. I learned to endure the uncomfortable showers. I always got in from the yard on time. And, I never drew attention to myself. But I still planned to run the first chance I got. Hatred for Brother McCormack grew darker in my heart.

Then Mom appeared in my classroom. "Come on you're leaving," She said

Just like that. In an instant, I was free. The car waited in the courtyard, just where it sat weeks before. On the way home I told Mom everything that happened.

"I'm so sorry" she said.

"I didn't know. I called the school and asked them if what you said was true. And they denied it. I talked to The Marstons, who couldn't believe it. I even talked to the Sheriff who thought the place was a good place for delinquents. But, I believed you. I'll never send you away again. I promise. After all, you're only a kid once." She said.

Chapter 11

The Little Trailer Park

No one was surprised when Mom announced her engagement to Virgil. Wedding plans were made and Mom brought home lovely studio photos of the new couple. They looked great together. The wedding soon followed. They chose to be married before a justice of the peace with a couple of witnesses and no family. After a short honeymoon, Mom packed our belongings into Virgil's car. Our new home was Virgil's 1948 Zimmer trailer house. I was amazed at how much could be crammed into a home eight feet wide and twenty-eight feet long. It was parked in the small Airline Trailer Park just off Highway 99, two blocks south of 188th Street, in the community of Bow Lake.

Ronnie Olson was in my room at school and we were already good friends. Now we were neighbors. He and his little brother Charley lived through the woods on 188th Street. Their tiny one-room house sat on the remains of an old family farm. A grown over trail followed an abandoned road through the woods from behind the trailer park, to where it became the Olson's drive way.

Just above the road by the Olson's house stood two ancient cherry trees. When summer arrived and the sun sneaked its warm light thought the clouds, the cherries ripened. Two boys sat happily in a treetop reaching high to the ripest fruit. Ronnie and I talked and ate, observing the country from our perch. Charley wasn't much of a climber; he was only six years old, so he stuck to lower branches, where the cherries weren't as ripe. It was good that he did. He had fallen out of the tree earlier and bruised himself. From our high branches we could see the front of the Olson's tiny house and watch Charley and his collie wandering around the yard as we stained our clothes with cherry juice and pitch. The collie never left Charley alone. Once when Charley did something to cause his dad to come running out of the house and turn Charley over his knee, the dog attacked Mister Olson. Charley was safe with his dog.

On the third day of cherry eating, Ronny got sick. He quit the tree and disappeared into the outhouse. When he came back he was through with cherries. Too bad about Ronny, I kept climbing higher for the best cherries. Then I got a cramp. By the time I got out of the tree, I too was sick. Ronny was back in the outhouse that I suddenly needed. I grabbed my bike, and peddled as fast as I could along the forest trail. I braked hard, letting the bike fall to the ground as I dashed into the washhouse toilet just in time.

Charley never got sick. His fall kept him out of the tree. By the time the cherries had ripened to where they could be reached from the ground, no one was interested.

That summer, Virgil took Mom and me on a trip to Minnesota. Somewhere along the way I heard Mom tell Virgil. "It's too bad Paul's too young to remember this trip."

The Little Trailer Park

She was right. But I did remember how US highway 10 twisted with hairpin turns and switchbacks as we crept between tall trees and rocky cliffs in the Snoqualmie Pass. Just beyond the Pass was the small town of Cle Elum that clung to the highway for its sustenance. The town grew up around logging and coal mining. As the natural resources declined, automobile traffic increased, providing a new source of income. Highway 10 was the main street of town. Gas stations and restaurants catered to travelers, and the town was busy.

Traffic was thick the Saturday morning we drove through town. Impatient motorists pressed toward the open road by going over the twenty-five-mile-an-hour speed limit. About half way through town, a red light flashed in our rear window. Virgil pulled off to the side of the road, and waited for the cop to walk up to his window.

"I wasn't speeding. I was going the same speed as everyone else." Virgil said.

"But, you were still speeding."

After a useless argument, the cop said. "Follow me to the court house. You can tell it to the judge."

Virgil had to pay his ticket immediately or sit it out in jail. The hundred dollars in his wallet for the trip, was now ten dollars lighter. Virgil complained for miles.

The landscape soon became barren as we drove away from the mountains. We crept through the town of Ellensburg at the posted speed limit, while Virgil continued to berate the cop in Cle Elum, and any other cop that might be hiding behind a billboard. Soon the highway twisted its way down miles of sage brushed mountainside that led to the Columbia River. We crossed a narrow bridge with the great Columbia River flowing fast beneath us, and still Virgil griped about his undeserved fine. As we climbed back out of the river canyon, Mom had heard enough.

"I don't want to hear any more about your speeding ticket," She insisted.

But, that didn't end the complaining. As we drove through the desert of Eastern Washington the tone of our trip was set. Suddenly a large dust devil crossed the highway in front of us. It hit a pickup truck in front of us, causing it to swerve.

"My God, it's a tornado," Mom yelled.

I grabbed hold of the back of the seat.

"That's just a dust devil," Virgil said.

"A dust devil, what's a dust devil? Mom asked.

"It's a whirlwind," Virgil said.

"A whirlwind? Did you see what it did to that pickup?"

The dust devil incident replaced the cop incident until something else caused a new disagreement. I settled down and enjoyed the passing scenery.

We crept through Spokane, a city of red brick buildings, and then, ninety miles past Spokane we started up a steep slope leading to Look Out Pass in the Rocky Mountains. It was mid afternoon and it was hot. As we gained elevation, we saw cars steaming from their radiators. Occasionally a car was stopped by the road with a plume of steam rising above it.

The Little Trailer Park

Before long our car began to boil over too.

At the summit of the pass was a rustic gas station. Motorists were lined up for water. Cars were parked in a gravel lot with the hoods up giving off steam. Prewar cars didn't have sealed water systems, so when the water got hot, it just evaporated until there wasn't enough to cool the engine and it boiled over. Some cars carried canvas bags of water hung around a radiator cap or headlight, for spare water.

The gas station had a wooden signpost with arrows pointing in all directions. Each arrow reported the distance to some far off destination, like Missoula, Seattle or New York.

We left the station and wound our way through Montana and on to North Dakota. Somewhere near the Badlands a new road was under construction that was taking the kinks out of the old road we were following.

Before long, I was standing in Grandma Strand's Kitchen. It seemed much smaller than I remembered. Upstairs in the little bedroom, my paper soldiers were laying under the window, right where I left them years earlier. I also remember standing where our little home had burned years ago. My pedal car still stood in the yard. Mom was right I wouldn't remember much about the trip. I don't remember anything else, or the trip home.

When we got back, Virgil left for Alaska. His welding skills were important to national defense. He went to the small, but vital island of Adak in the Aleutian Island chain. This five mile wide island was a military airbase, strategically located halfway between North America and Asia. His letters home told of winds and heavy rainfall. In one photo, a metal runway was rolled up by the wind.

In July, Mom and Mavis took waitress jobs at the Seattle - Tacoma International Airport. In 1950 the airport had only two major buildings, The Northwest Airlines hanger and the brand new Central Terminal building. The restaurant was on the second floor where a glass wall presented a panoramic view of the Olympic Mountains and the runways below. The Seattle-Tacoma International Airport was recognized as the most modern and beautiful air terminal in the world. Northwest Orient Stratocruisers, with their big red tails, could be seen on the runways. Ironically, these big airplanes stopped on the little island of Adak for refueling on their way to the orient.

Mom loved her job. She bragged about her generous tips and some of the celebrities she chatted with; people like the young Billy Graham and my hero, Roy Rogers. There were others whose names didn't stick in my memory.

I started fifth grade that fall. Ronny and Rodney Forester were both in my room. So were a couple of white haired Norwegian brothers who couldn't speak English. We were glad to help them learn. On the playground we taught them to call our teacher a witch. We also replaced some other common words with our own not so nice substitutes. These were smart boys, they learned fast. After a few days they wouldn't come near us.

The Little Trailer Park

Our teacher was a rather skinny Mrs. Johnson who became well known around school when one of her breasts slid down to her waist while she stood in front of the class. She didn't seem to notice, and kept on teaching as if this was a common event. The classroom filled with snickers and giggles, but she paid no attention. By the next day the whole school was talking about Mrs. Johnson's falsies.

Our classroom was lined with books and served as our school library. That meant we had to go to other rooms occasionally while Mrs. Johnson became a librarian. Ironically, one of the other places was a bookmobile. Every week I checked out books, but never read them. About the only thing I did read was comics and Popular Science magazine. That was okay with Mom. After all, "you're only a child once."

One of the other rooms was the basement music room. It was small and unimpressive but it had a record player. Our teacher told us about a Peruvian native singer called Yma Sumac. Then she played the record. I was enthralled by the most beautiful voice I ever heard and longed to hear her again.

Back in my classroom I could see the entire airport through my schoolroom window. It was comforting that I could see where my mom worked, any time I wanted to look. I also watched the airplanes take off and land.

When Grandpa Was a Kid

Chapter 12

The Cougar

This was the winter of the cougar. It started in the damp drizzle of a fall evening. Rodney Forester lived only two trailers away. Naturally he and I started hanging out together around the trailer court. One night Rod and I heard a blood chilling scream carry up from the highway. We ran to the edge of the trailer park and down to highway 99. We thought a car had hit a woman, but we didn't see anyone. There were just cars going past. We decided to cross over to the swampy woods on the other side and take a look. Then I stopped and grabbed Rod's arm. A chill ran up my back.

"You ever hear a woman scream like that?" I said.

"No." he said.

"I think it sounds like a cougar."

We consulted a retired neighbor, Chief. He was the same guy who came to see us after the earthquake. He said he thought that cougars and bears were coming closer to population because there was more snow in the hills than usual for this time of year, and they were looking for food.

With that incident behind us Rod and I moved on to other concerns as the days shortened.

Rod showed me his small stamp collection. They were beautiful little prints, like a museum gallery hung in a book. The next time Mom took me to Seattle I saw envelopes of stamps at the large Woolworth store on

Third and Pike. I bought an envelope of one hundred American stamps. I studied each one. The next time I went to Woolworth's I picked up a stamp collector's kit with an American stamp album, stamp hinges, tweezers, magnifying glass and a stock book. I put all my stamps in the album. My spares went into the stock book. I looked for more.

I asked around to see if friends and neighbors would give me old envelopes. Some did. I added them to my collection. Then I struck pay dirt. The back pages of a Popular Science magazine advertized stamps. I mailed away for offers from the Mystic Stamp Company, The Harrison Stamp Company and some others. They gave me free stamps, if I would review stamps they sent to me on approval. My collection started getting serious.

Another source of stamps was the Hisken Stamp and Coin store on Second Avenue in Seattle. There I could study stamps and ask questions about stamp collecting. I also bought a few stamps. My collection began to hold some semi-rare eighteenth and nineteenth century stamps. It included practically all of the common twentieth century stamps.

Each stamp had a story to tell, like the stamp with a picture of four chaplains who once gave up their seats in the lifeboats. They sacrificed their lives so others could survive the sinking of a troop ship during the war. My collection became a regular source of pleasure.

As Christmas approached I went with Mom to Seattle by bus for shopping and movies. Everything

The Cougar

was looking like Christmas. On the bus home, Mom said we weren't going to have a Christmas tree.

"Why not?" I wanted to know.

"There's no room for one." she said.

"Not even a small one?"

"No."

One evening on our way home from school I told Rodney of Mom's treeless Christmas idea. As we talked I saw a Douglas fir seedling growing in the ditch alongside the highway.

"I got me a Christmas tree". I said.

Rodney looked skeptical.

It was two feet tall but looked like a Christmas tree to me. I pulled out my pocket knife and cut it off. When Mom came home, she acted like it was the nicest little tree she ever saw, and then decorated it. We had a Christmas tree.

Chief's theory about more snow in the low lands came true when a good 20 inches of snow fell in January, setting an all time one-month record. Records for the coldest weather were also broken. School was out, roads were closed, airplanes were grounded and people were trapped in the mountain passes. Highway 99 was piled high on each side with tall snow banks. We lived close enough to the airport that Mom and Mavis could walk to work. One night when Mavis opened the door, she was covered with snow and dirt. She said she was walking along highway 99 on her way home from her waitress job at the airport, when she heard the roar of a snowplow right behind her. The snowplow didn't see her. She leapt out of the way, landing in piled up snow down in the swampy woods below. The snowplow threw more snow down on top of her as it passed. We almost lost Mavis that night.

Paul and Mavis by the trailer. with Charley Olson's dog

This terrible winter was a child's dream. The earth was white -- a deep beautiful white. We made snowmen and snow forts. Snowball fights lasted all day. In the evening, my wet mittens lay steaming on our little oil stove that kept us cozy and warm on cold winter nights. Our trailer, built in Michigan, was well insulated

But some trailers weren't insulated at all, and required constant heating. One night while Rodney and I wandered around in the snow we saw a glowing red hole in the side of a very small trailer. The trailer was on fire. We banged on the door but the old man who lived there didn't answer. We ran yelling, "fire, fire." Rodney's parents came running and broke into the trailer. So did Chief. Chief was called Chief because he was a retired fireman. Soon a fire truck came. The old man who lived in the trailer, had died before the fire started. He was cooking dinner with the stove on high. Eventually the overheated stove ignited the trailer.

One night, while I was crunching through the

The Cougar

snow to the washhouse, I heard something over my head that stopped my breath. With a quick glance up, I saw a cougar crouched on a large branch above the washhouse. I turned and ran the short distance back to the trailer. I burst in and slammed the door. Mom and Mavis were sitting on the couch.

"There's a cougar over at the washhouse," I said.

"A what?" Mom said.

"I saw a cougar on a branch above the door."

"There can't be a cougar over the washhouse."

"There is," I insisted.

They didn't believe me. At night I lay in the quiet listening for the cougar. Rodney and I no longer wandered around in the dark.

One evening after school when the snow had melted, a friend and I went into the swampy woods behind his house. We were standing beside the Des Moines Creek. My friend was telling me how he caught salmon minnows. I was looking at raccoon tracks in the sand by the creek. Then I saw a cougar track.

"Look at this," I said. "It's a cougar track, and it's fresh."

"There's some more," my friend said."

I looked up and saw the silhouette of a cougar in the bushes down the creek a ways.

"There it is!" I gasped.

My friend saw it too. We scrambled up two small alder trees and looked at each other through the bare limbs.

"I can't see the cougar," I said.

"Maybe it ran off."

"We can't stay here."

We jumped down from the trees, and ran for the closest shelter. We ducked into a well house on my friend's property and slammed the door.

"An old guy in the trailer park, said cougars come down in the winter to look for food," I said.

My friend made it clear that we had to get going. "We can't stay in here long. The sun's going down."

I peeked out the door. There was no sign of the cougar. We crept out and headed for his house.

I kept on going. I had to get home. There were two ways I could go, the shortcut through the swampy woods or the long way down 192nd Street. I walked along 192nd Street. I didn't take my eyes off the woods. When I got to Highway 99, I crossed over and went home. Mom was there.

"I saw the cougar again. It was by the creek over in the woods across from school," I said.

"Well, maybe. Just don't go in those woods anymore."

"Don't worry, I won't!"

It seemed to me that the cougar could be anywhere. That night every noise from outside sounded like a cougar. My thoughts began to torture me. *What if it hides under the trailer? Is it on the roof?* Then I began to doubt myself. *Did I really see a cougar? What if it was something else?* That night I went to sleep saying my prayers.

The next day I confronted Mom. "Why don't you believe me that I saw a cougar?"

The Cougar

"Maybe you did, and maybe you didn't," she said.

"A boy's imagination can seem very real, especially if you're scared."

Then she told me to sit down so she could tell me a story.

"When your father and I were first married, he used to walk home from work along a gravel road cut through the wilderness. It went past our cabin. Sometimes I liked to walk along the road to meet him. One evening I heard some rustling in the bushes by the side of the road. Well, your dad and I used to play little tricks on each other, so I said, 'okay you can come out now.'

But he stayed quiet and kept walking through the brush.

'That's enough, you better come out or I'm coming in after you,' I called.

Still nothing. So I grabbed a handful of gravel from the road to throw at him. When I bent down I saw your dad just coming into sight down the road. I froze. Then I yelled, 'Cliff, hurry, there's something in the woods.'

He heard me and began trotting toward me.

'What's the matter?' He yelled.

Then a huge black cat jumped across the road ahead of me in a single bound. It never even touched the road. By the time your dad and I met we were both running. If your dad hadn't come when he did, I could have been attacked. If I hadn't set out to meet him, he could have been attacked.

"I don't know if anyone believed our story, but

Someone was watching over us. Later, I found out a circus train had crashed over by Moose Lake. Among the missing animals was a black panther."

Mom understood.

Of all of my childhood birthdays, I can remember only two; one at Briscoe, and one with Mavis. Mom was at the airport waiting tables and wouldn't be home until late. There was no cake or ice cream. But Mavis took two white Hostess Snowballs and put them each on a saucer. Mine had a lighted candle. She set them on the little kitchen table, and then sang Happy Birthday to me. I turned eleven.

When summer came, Rodney moved away. Mom heard back from his mother that their trailer house came loose while they were going up a hill. They looked back to see it coasting backward. They gave chase, but it disappeared around a corner. Then, when they reached the bottom of the hill, they saw their trailer parked neatly in the front row of a trailer sales lot.

Vacation Bible School started at the Angle Lake Presbyterian Church. I signed up and brought Ronny with me. The highlight of the week was a day of swimming and rubber band powered boat racing at Angle Lake. Ronny and I built rubber band powered paddleboats. They were simple to make. I knew how because my dad made one for me when I was little.

At the lake, the pastor had a finish line set up near the shore. We waded out with our boats and lined them up in the water pointing toward the finish line. Paul Boynton, a kid I remembered from Sunny Dale

The Cougar

School, had a sleek, narrow, boat with a brass propeller, powered by a long rubber band wound into tight knots below the polished boat. It looked professionally made. When the pastor yelled go my boat paddled slowly in a circle. The rest of the boats did about the same, but Boynton's boat dashed straight across the finish line with no competition.

The competitors whispered, "His dad probably made it for him."

I discovered a source of income. Empty beer and pop bottles were refundable. I could sell beer bottles for one cent each, and three cents for quart bottles. Pop bottles varied by size up to a nickel. I walked along Highway 99 and gathered empties thrown from cars. I knew where the drunks lived and could find bottles sitting around their trailers and in parking lots, sometimes by the case. By Saturday morning I usually had enough for a trip into Seattle. Ronny Olson and sometimes Pat Colacurcio came with me. Pat lived on a farm across 188th from Ronny and also attended Angle Lake School.

In town we went to the Kress 5 and 10 cent store, Woolworths and the movies. Just up the street from the Hisken Stamp and Coin store was a hotel owned by Pat's brother Frank. His sister Rose ran the kitchen. When we came in she served us a plate of ravioli -- a first for Ronny and me.

Seattle had plenty of theaters. Saturday matinees were especially for kids, with cartoons and serialized adventures. The main feature was often a cowboy movie, but with a little luck it was Tarzan or Abbot and

Costello.

One afternoon after seeing a movie called King Solomon's Mines, we wanted to emulate the movie's trip through the African savanna and go on safari. We decided to hunt for the cougar. Little neighbor kids from the trailer park joined us. They were eager to track a cougar through the wilderness. We got together in an old chicken coup and planned. Ronny and I would lead the party and the little kids would be bearers. But we needed weapons.

Bracken ferns grew high on long stalks, then dried hard. The end that pulled from the ground was shaped like a spear point. We picked and trimmed bracken ferns until we had bundles of them. With Ronny in the lead, we marched off single file with hands full of spears. Our safari led us through tall dry grass to the edge of the woods. We carefully parted the branches as we moved quietly into an alder grove, walking single file, like in the movie. Charley's collie acted as rear guard.

"Where are we going?" Charley asked.

"Shhh, we're following a cougar," Ronny Said.

We slowly moved deeper into the grove.

"I'm scared," some little kid said.

"Don't worry, it's just pretend," Ronny said.

"I see it! I see it!" Another little kid shouted.

The little kids dropped their spears and ran yelling from the woods. Ronny and I did the same. I doubt if anyone saw a cougar, but the fear was real.

As the summer dragged on we found things to keep us busy. One activity lasted all summer. Ronny,

The Cougar

Charley and I, and any other boys that came around, would have pissing contests. It started because the Olson's had an outdoor toilet. It was easier to duck behind the outhouse to take a leak than to go inside. The contest was to see who could piss the farthest up the wall. There was also a clump of grass that we pissed on to see how well it would grow. By the time the orchard grass turned brown and died, our clump of grass was green and stood taller than Charley.

That fall, Virgil came home. His head touched the ceiling of the trailer, causing him to bend his neck a little. He reached into his pocket and handed me all the change he had. I had to hold out both hands. I left for the Bow Lake Gas and Grocery.

Not long after school started Virgil announced that he took a job in Eastern Washington doing something with atomic energy. Mavis had already moved out and had a job as a telephone operator in Seattle. We had to move again. I wanted to stay with my friends, but that wasn't for me to decide.

When Grandpa Was a Kid

Chapter 13

The Big Trailer Park

Virgil's 1941 Plymouth was packed and our trailer house was ready to go when Virgil's friend, Bill Thompson, showed up with his Chevy pick-up. He backed up to the trailer tongue, set the hitch on the towing ball, and secured it with two chains. Bill slowly pulled the trailer loose. The truck and trailer squeaked down the gravel drive and onto highway 99. We were on our way to Richland.

Any trip east from Western Washington is a trip through the Cascade Mountains. A string of volcanoes stand above the rest of the mountains, with Mount Rainier crowning the range at 14,410 feet. At Washington's northern latitude, snow fills the mountains from late fall to mid spring. These mountains divide the state into two separate and distinct regions, not just geographically, but politically, socially and meteorologically.

We took the narrow, curved White Pass that skirts Mount Rainier. In early October the road was clear, so Bill wasted no time speeding our home through the mountains and into the desert beyond.

We stopped at a roadside restaurant for a late dinner somewhere east of Yakima. During dinner, the adults sipped red cocktails in tall frosted glasses.

"Do you think I could have one of those," I asked?

The waitress said, "sure" and brought me a tall frosted glass filled with red sparkling pop and a maraschino cherry. She called it a Roy Rogers.

I liked everything about Roy Rogers, making my drink even better.

After dinner, we resumed our trip with Bill in the lead and Virgil, Mom and I following in the Plymouth.

It was exciting to watch the truck and trailer house as it sped ahead of us across the dark desert. Occasional tumbleweeds rolled through our headlights. We had to speed to keep up because Bill never slowed down. He scared Mom.

"Everything we own is in that trailer", she pleaded with Virgil, "Can't you get him to be more careful?"

We arrived late but it didn't take long to position the trailer and plug in its single electric cord. In the morning our trailer was parked on the corner of 900-H. That meant we lived on H Street in the 900 block of the largest trailer park on earth.

North Richland with 3,600 trailers

Our lot was only about 25 feet wide and 40 feet deep. On one side was a wooden carport-like structure with six four-by-four legs and a tarpapered roof. Our trailer sat under it, just like everybody else's. There were over 3,600 of these little lots lined up in rows, and divided into blocks by cross streets. The streets were blacktop continuing to narrow blacktop sidewalks on each side. Mom unpacked and decorated our little

The Big Trailer Park

home with doilies and flowers, just like it was before we moved.

There were all sizes of trailers; small, smaller and smallest. The biggest ones weren't much over 30 feet long and none were greater than 8 feet wide. The smallest ones could have been 10 feet long. None of them had bathrooms. There was a bathhouse in the center of each block for toileting and bathing, with a laundry room for everyone's wringer washers.

There was a kind of status among trailer dwellers. At the top of the list were Spartan Manors and Spartan Mansions, made by the Spartan Aircraft Company in Oklahoma. They were gorgeous, made of polished aluminum with big wrap around front windows and port holes in the doors. Our 1948 Zimmer was mediocre, with the status of being built in the east were trailers were well insulated. California built trailers weren't up to the cold desert winters.

Virgil got up early in the morning and joined the lines of men walking to the buses that would take them to what we called, "the Area". They were construction workers. Dozens of them filed passed our trailer. Hundreds more came out of every street in the trailer park. It was exciting to watch them move through the pre-dawn. Some went straight to the gates of the Area, where buses waited to take them to work, others went to one of the large cafeterias for breakfast, first.

The Area was actually several areas, collectively called the Hanford Nuclear Reservation. It was established in 1943 during World War II as part of the Manhattan Project to provide the plutonium necessary for the development of nuclear weapons. Hanford produced the plutonium used in the bomb that destroyed Nagasaki. The cold war kept production going, as the nation needed even more plutonium for more bombs, so we could blow the Soviet Union farther into oblivion than they could us.

The government chose this place because they wanted to create plutonium in a location as remote from population as possible and still have a railroad and other services, as well as air force protection, nearby. Hanford was reputed to be the best spot in the nation for this.

**Paul at home on the corner of 900 H
1 of 3,600 trailers**

The remoteness was visible. Stunted sage brush and clumps of grass carpeted the desert vistas to the horizon. Two large rivers, the Snake and Yakima, flowed into the Columbia just downstream of Richland. High above it stretched the Majestic Rattlesnake Ridge. The beauty of this land was a marvel of creation.

We lived in North Richland, which was part of the Hanford Nuclear Reservation. The community included a commissary, drugstore, gas station, firehouse, movie theater, a huge barbershop, a school, a park, and maybe a couple of services I forgot about. There were also men's and women's dormitories, army barracks and several very large cafeterias. Mom

The Big Trailer Park

worked in one of the cafeterias for awhile. She let me eat there. It was fun to mix with so many people and choose my own food from the serving line. The buildings sat neatly on straight gridded streets.

Only three or four miles across the desert and down river, was Richland, an unincorporated town managed by General Electric for the Atomic Energy Commission, just like everything else they managed for the government. Some 22,000 people lived there in 1951. (More than 50,000 if North Richland was included.) Even though Richland belonged to the government, it was a real town and looked like one. It had a full complement of stores, a hospital, schools, and emergency services. Richland even had one of the nation's first shopping centers, called Uptown Richland. It had things I liked; a theater, a hobby shop, an ice cream store and a Spudnut shop. Spudnuts were fluffy soft doughnuts that included some form of potato in the recipe. There were no better doughnuts.

The houses were a little odd, but organized. The Army Corps of Engineers and some contractors started building them during the war, using several basic plans. In 1943, houses started popping out of the desert dust to accommodate the influx of an army of civilian workers.

Housing styles were identified by letter codes. People lived in "A" duplexes or "F" houses and so on. The letters designated size, from one to four bedrooms, single house or duplex. Social status was built into the layout of the streets and positioning of the houses, allowing big shots to live near big shots and lesser workers to be near their peers. The whole place was planned to provide emergency and adequate housing, while at the same time, engineering social bliss. They were all mansions compared to our housing. North Richland was the emergency part, but I liked it. This planned "village", as they called it, was repeated in Oak Ridge and Los Alamos, but Richland was the largest.

Within days of our arrival the wind began to blow. The air filled with everything light enough for the wind to grab, and plenty of dust. Big tumbleweeds bounced through the streets and lodged against trailers, cars and fences. They piled up in yards and in the playgrounds. Our trailer shook, then glass shattered and a garbage can lid wedged itself in our small front window. We would see more windstorms and more garbage can lids flying through the air. The wind blew from the Pacific Ocean, gaining force as it narrowed through the Columbia River Gorge, between Washington and Oregon, then on to Richland.

Virgil's contribution toward building nuclear weapons was Heliarc welding. His skills were in demand and his wages were excellent. He showed us one of his weekly paychecks.

"Look at this", he said, "a hundred and ten bucks, take home pay."

Gas was about twenty-three cents a gallon and bread was about twenty cents a loaf. Virgil liked to bank his money and he paid cash for everything.

He said that during the war he told his buddies, "When I get out, I'm going to have a new house and a

The Big Trailer Park

new car -- paid for."

Mom found work at a busy drugstore café that included a soda fountain. I loved to go in and see Mom smiling and happy in her pretty uniform. She sometimes made a strawberry ice-cream soda for me, my favorite.

I enrolled in the sixth grade at the John Ball elementary School, there in the trailer park. The school was constructed of several classroom sized Quonset huts attached to a long rectangular hall with asbestos insulated steam pipes hanging from the ceiling.

What I heard about atomic bombs and doomsday became foremost in my mind. We lived within sight of a nuclear reactor that made the prime ingredients for atomic bombs, and there were more beyond the horizon. We were a target. Soviet airplanes could reach us, and they now had their own bomb. We could be destroyed like the films showed; with a white hot light blinding or cooking us, then the blast wave tearing us apart and spreading our ashes across an indifferent desert.

Our school kept this fear fresh. They wanted us to survive an atomic bomb attack. A trench was dug in the sand, the length of the school. During air raid drills, we had to run and jump, face down, into the trench, and do it in two minutes or less. We then laid there waiting for the drill to end or the white flash to come. I couldn't help remembering the words of a movie I saw in Winlock that ended with, "Is this the beginning or the end?"

I don't remember any community drills. I guess

only school kids were expected to survive the attack. The school teachers didn't seem to care either. They came to the trench, but never laid down.

The rest of school was just plain boring. But, luck would have it, I sat right next to one of the few tiny windows on the Quonset hut wall. The view was bad, so I spent some time looking at the blackboard. I didn't understand what the class was doing and it didn't do any good to ask. One day I watched the teacher put some long division problems on the board, but I couldn't figure them out, so I turned back to the window. Then I heard the heavy footed Mrs. Johnson coming down my row banging her feet on the wooden floor yelling, "Paul! Paul!"

I froze and gaped at her as she grabbed the other Paul in the next row. I didn't know what he did to deserve so much attention. In a little while I returned to my window.

There was a larger multi-purpose Quonset hut down the hall where physical education classes were held when the weather was bad. They set up a record player and played county music while we learned to square dance.

The record went something like, "Bow to your partner, bow to your corner ... allemande left with your left hand ... and promenade."

We all ran around the room doing whatever the record told us to do. After a long cold winter we could square dance.

Making friends was easy. We were all new. On my block I had two friends, a roundish sort of kid at

The Big Trailer Park

the other end of the block, named Galen who loved to laugh, and a tall slim kid, named Billy, who was smart beyond his age. I watched him sketch the plans for a model speed boat and build it. He lived next to the play ground across the street with his four brothers and a sister. Their trailer was only two feet longer than ours. Trailer houses were very creative about providing sleeping space, but I'm sure they couldn't all sit at the table at the same time. Billy had a shed behind the trailer for a bedroom, heated only with a space heater. It was common for bigger boys to live in sheds.

Christmas was a weapons holiday. Several kids got rifles that shot ping pong balls, some got BB guns, but worst of all were the bows and arrows. The kids who got those, stood in the play ground and shot them straight in the air, making other kids watch the sky while scrambling to save their lives. The arrows soon disappeared.

That winter I took a paper route delivering the Spokane Chronicle. I got the 600 block. It was one block wide and about 12 blocks deep, where only black families were relegated to live. I hadn't experienced segregation before, but it was a way of life in Richland. Many of the people who came to North Richland were from places where segregation was the norm, and they carried their cultural imperatives with them. But like everyone else, the people in the segregated block came to work in the Area. My customers were all black but the services they received were provided by white people; a white paper boy, white milkman, white mail man and so on. But in public places not every white person would provide them a service.

Where Mom grew up in Northern Minnesota, the Indians were segregated to the point of misery or even death. Mom truly hated that, and tolerated no racism. When she saw black customers turned away at the café where she worked, she made sure she served them. I didn't think much about racism, but some of the dogs in the 600 block really scared me.

On garbage day a cornucopia of unwanted stuff lay by the street. I took my bike with a wagon tied to the back, and dragged home a wooden packing crate that I could use to build a small shed behind our trailer. I found enough other material to add a front wall with a window and door, plus a carpet, a long extension cord, for electricity, some other odds and ends, and even a radio. The shed was only about 4 feet high, and deep by maybe five feet. It faced "H" Street, where the newspaper distributor dropped my bundle. I sat in it and folded my papers for delivery. I later started selling papers to workers as they got off the busses from the Area. That was easier and exciting. Papers sold fast -- cash in hand.

I began reading the paper. I learned about the Korean War and followed the maps provided almost every day. I read about MIG ally and the dog fights between Russian MIG-15s and American F86s. I admired war planes and identified all the fighters and inceptors involved. One evening the paper had a half page picture of General MacArthur saying, "Old soldiers never die, they just fade away." I felt closer to

The Big Trailer Park

the war.

When spring arrived, so did yo-yos, marbles and movies. Most boys had yo-yos. we stood around for hours practicing until some of us were doing the cradle, walk the dog, and 'round the world. We even had a yo-yo demonstration at school. The yo-yo of choice was a Duncan Professional. Sometimes a string would break sending the yo-yo flying into anything or anybody that got in the way. They were confiscated at school. After mine flew apart at home, Mom forbade me to use it anywhere near the trailer.

"Get away from the house with that thing, you could break a window!"

She didn't appreciate how good I was getting with my yo-yo.

Soon, marbles became the number one pastime for boys. It was a form of gambling. The most popular game was a large circle scratched on smooth dirt. Each player placed marbles in the center. A special marble called a shooter was used to try and hit marbles and knock them out of the circle. Any marbles knocked out of the circle became the property of the kid who knocked them out. Some kids won large numbers of marbles. My mom crocheted marble bags for me and my friends.

The game of marbles was approved by the school and we played marbles at recess. Sanctioned contests were held, complete with championship playoffs. One of the kids in my room won a new Schwinn bicycle.

Mom allowed me to go to movies by myself. I would either go to the theater in North Richland or catch the army bus to the theater in Uptown Richland. Movies changed frequently enough that I could go once or twice a week. One movie, The Third Man, had a haunting theme that ran throughout the movie, played only on a zither.

One Saturday, some friends and I joined a bunch of other trailer park kids at the North Richland Theater to watch Jimmy Stewart in Winchester 76. When the movie ended, we went down to the arroyos by the Columbia River and acted out the movie, using our BB guns. The fun ended when some other kids took pot-shots at us. We shot back, but got out of there before we got hurt.

Some other trouble came our way one Saturday when we decided to get a closer look at the nearest reactor. All that separated us from the Area was a good barbed wire fence and some ignorable warning signs. We crawled under the fence and crept through the brush, Indian style, keeping low like in the movies. A few hundred feet out, a small airplane came toward us. It circled and a load speaker addressed us. We were told to get out "right now."

I saw a gun sticking out of the plane that circled around us. We ran for the fence and safety. Then the plane flew away.

Richland created a couple of strange laws regarding kids. Some kids at school ate Kool Aid straight from the package. This was thought to be harmful, so laws were passed making it illegal to sell Kool Aid to kids. Then paperback books were deemed to be too mature for kids, and we couldn't buy those

The Big Trailer Park

either. Up to then, I only read comic books, Popular Science magazine and newspapers, so this new ban peaked my interest. I began looking through paperbacks to see why they were banned I was not a good student and didn't read much, but now I was reading mature paperback novels including one titled, The Big Rape This was surely the banned literature I was looking for. I was disappointed that all I found was a story about the rape of Berlin by its Russian conquerors.

Mavis sent me stamps for my collection, and introduced me to collecting stamps in "plate blocks of four", which I began buying at the post office, for three cents a stamp. Sometime that year, she came to stay with us for a while, but I don't remember why or how long she stayed. I thought she was working somewhere in Seattle

Summer came. I stayed home a lot, mostly with Mom but sometimes alone. It was always good to be home with Mom, she went about her work singing and dancing around our little trailer and listening to popular music on the radio. Songs like, "The Tennessee Waltz" and "Mockingbird Hill" played while she sang along, "When the sun in the morning peeps over the hill, and kisses the roses 'round my window sill...on Mockingbird Hill." Mom sounded better than the radio as she danced around preparing supper for her family.

Life was good although Virgil and Mom groused at each other a lot. Mom didn't like his constant questioning about what she was doing.

When Grandpa Was a Kid

The trailer got hot, so I spent much of each day riding my bike around the neighborhood just to be outdoors. One day I was riding my bike through the streets and lollygagging around talking to people, when a woman said she was moving.

"I can't take my dog." She told me.

"What kind of dog is it?" I was quick to ask.

She returned with a small black mixed Pomeranian.

"Her name is Bobby. Do you want her?" she asked.

"I have to ask my mom."

She let me put the dog in my basket and I rode home to show Mom.

Mom said, "Of course you can have the dog. You're only a child once."

Bobby and I became pals. She slept on my bed at night and rode in the basket as I peddled my bike around the camp. Mom took a quick liking to the little dog. She called her "Flea Bag."

We didn't keep Bobby fenced in. Most little dogs just ran freely through the neighborhood. On hot days, when she wasn't stretched out under the trailer, she liked to sit and gaze into the distance. One afternoon I

The Big Trailer Park

saw her sitting on the street in front of the trailer. A car was coming.

I yelled, "Bobby! Bobby!"

The car kept coming.

"Here, Bobby!"

Then the car ran right over her.

"Bobby, no!"

But the car was high enough to pass over her and she remained sitting just as before. I scooped Bobby up and vowed to watch her more carefully.

It began to rain. I'll never forget how sweet and fresh the desert smelled and felt after a summer rain. It filled my nostrils with cool moisture and the scent of damp earth and sage brush. Only those who have experienced this desert phenomenon understand its refreshing qualities, and will long to experience it again.

Kids have little or no part in the decisions that affect their lives. Unbenounced to me, Virgil took a new job working for his friend Bill Thompson in Seattle. He and Mom paid cash for a small house in Midway Washington, just a block off of Highway 99. We were going to move again.

Always moving; always the new kid, always behind in school, always un-trusted. Life would have to start all over again. I didn't want to be the new kid anymore. I knew the trailer park was temporary but I thought it go on forever.

When Grandpa Was a Kid

Chapter 14

Midway

It was early summer 1951 when we pulled into the yard of our new home in Midway, Washington. It was called Midway because it was sixteen miles south of Seattle and sixteen miles north of Tacoma. It was also between the waterfront town of Des Moines and the busy little framing town of Kent. Our new home sat on a narrow half-acre of pasture that stretched from 30th Avenue to the back yard of Betty's cafe on Highway 99.

The house was new, but very small. It had just one bedroom with an L-shaped living room and kitchen combination. The inside was so bare that it didn't even have cupboards over the sink. But a small covered porch was welcoming.

We had no furniture so we all slept on the floor. This lasted until Mom and Virgil went to an auction. The following Saturday, a truck load of furniture arrived. Into the bedroom went a beautiful old inlayed and polished wood bedroom set. A chair and couch went into the living room and a dinette set with chrome legs and a red plastic top sat beside a real Frigidaire. We were Modern. Mom finished the decor with doilies, her chalk artwork and potted plants. Just like in the trailer, I would sleep on the couch.

During the night and early morning, we heard cars driving through our yard. It turned out that our house was built on a popular short cut to highway 99 and Betty's café. This continued even during the day, until Virgil's Plymouth parked in the middle of the shortcut made it clear that the house was occupied. I thought it was fun to watch the young men coming through our yard in their old cars. Some sped through way too fast, especially the one who lived across the street. Virgil put some wire fencing across the back of the lot and the through traffic ended.

Bobby had the run of the yard and sometimes beyond. Mom would just stick her head out of door and yell, "Bobby!" and the dog would saunter home.

One day she went out to call the dog and heard the neighbor lady across the road calling, "Bobby" at the same time. A tall skinny kid went running into the neighbor's house.

Mom and the neighbor lady walked out into the street and got acquainted. Her name was Zola Adams. Bobby was her fifteen-year old son. She also had a seventeen-teen year old son, Ernie, who I recognized from his trips through our yard. Her oldest son, Russ, was married and serving in the Navy. There were two married daughters living a few miles away. Her husband, Floyd, was at work. He was a cement finisher.

It didn't take me long to get to know Bobby, the neighbor boy, and his family. Their house was a small two story that looked homemade. The back had a covered porch where Zola did her laundry. Beyond that was an abandoned 1940 Ford, an old car frame, a couple of sheds, piles of used lumber, a scattering of rabbit hutches, and lots of other stuff. An expanse of forest hid it all from sight. The inside of the house was almost as cluttered.

We were only there a couple of weeks when Virgil's friend, Bill Thompson, came over talking about cars. He and Virgil hatched a plan to buy new cars directly from General Motors in Detroit. Virgil gave Bill enough money for a new Chevrolet, and then took him to the train station for his trip to Detroit. Cars were much cheaper where they were manufactured than from car dealers in the west. After a few days, Bill drove up in his new Chevrolet towing Virgil's new Maroon 1951 Chevrolet Powerglide, with a torpedo body. Virgil had fulfilled his dream, a new house and a new car – paid for.

Mavis started living with us. I don't remember why, but I do remember being bumped from the couch to a small bed hidden behind a large dresser in the corner of the bedroom with a blanket hung from the ceiling to make it more personal. This was actually a better arrangement since I slept different hours than the others. Mavis had a job in Seattle working for Allied Foods. She also had a boy friend, Bill something, who had a broad smile and a big loud motorcycle.

Mavis brought her piano with her. She was an accomplished piano player and often filled our little home with her music. I even learned to play a little. But I found other uses for her piano.

Mom's cat liked to walk on the keys. So before going to bed I sometimes opened the cover and waited for the cat to jump up on the piano. Sometimes when it did, Mom's voice came from the bedroom. "Paul did you leave the piano cover open?"

Yup, I thought. "I can't remember," I said.

"Would someone shut it please?"

Virgil wasn't as polite about it. He cursed the "damn" cat when he should have been yelling at me.

The cat had three kittens. I named them Hitler, Tojo and Mussolini. I spent hours arranging cardboard boxes for them to crawl through. Sometimes Bobby would lie down by the kittens with the perverted notion that she should nurse them.

But kittens don't stay kittens, and something had to be done with them. The decision was made that the kittens would be euthanized in a cardboard box fitted with a hose running from the exhaust pipe of Virgil's new Chevy. Everything was ready. Virgil started up the car. He raced the engine. Smoke rushed from the box. The kittens screamed in pain and terror.

Mom and Mavis stood horrified.

I started yelling. "Mom! Mom! Help! Virgil's killing the kittens! He's burning them to death!"

Mom had had enough. Not wanting to see anything in pain, except maybe Virgil, She stormed to the open car door. Virgil was pumping the accelerator.

"Stop that right now, you're torturing those poor kittens. What's the matter with you? Stop, Stop!" Mom yelled.

Virgil turned off the car and stomped into the house.

I pulled the smoking hot kittens from the box. They coughed and cried, but by the next day they were back playing again. They were eventually given away.

Midway

I soon found Zola to be a great cook. Her children and grandchildren showed up for Sunday dinner, and I was invited, probably because I hung around most of the day watching Zola cook. She made thick yellow dough and rolled it out flat, then cut it into thin strips to dry. She sent Ernie out to get a couple of rabbits. He killed them by grabbing them by the feet and hacking them hard in the neck, like a karate chop. Or would that be a rabbit punch? He then skinned and gutted them, and brought them to his mother. Dinner was homemade rabbit and noodle stew with bowls of other delicious foods made with baked beans, potatoes, vegetables and lots of boiled greens. There was more than plenty for everyone.

I became an occasional guest at that table and was thankful for it, but Zola startled me one day when she announced that, "Paul thinks of me as his mother. I'm his other mother."

I didn't know how to respond so I just grinned. Inside I was saying, *Don't tell people I like you more than my mom.* It made me feel like a traitor. But Zola was nice to me and fed me like I'd never eaten before.

Zola was also a good nurse. While killing time wandering around her back yard, I stepped down hard on a nail sticking out of one the many stray boards. I sat down and pulled the board away from my shoe exposing an inch of bloody nail. I hobbled toward the house yelling, "Zola. Zola. I stepped on a nail."

She took me to her front porch and sat me on a step, then carefully removed my shoe. Blood poured out. She left and came back with a bottle of rubbing alcohol. "Hold this right up against the hole." She instructed, and then went in the house.

I opened the bottle and applied the alcohol. It stung fierce but I did what I was told and pressed the open end of the bottle against the wound. I held it there for a long time, but she didn't come back. After a while, the alcohol was gone, sucked up into the nail hole – or so I thought. When Zola finally came back she said, "Let me see that foot."

I handed her the empty bottle and said, "It's all gone. It all went into my foot."

She took the bottle. "I don't think so."

Then she wrapped my foot and cleaned my shoe.

"Go home and wait for your mother," she said and went back into her house.

No one thought to take me to a doctor.

Zola was superstitious. One lazy summer afternoon she caught me standing idly rocking a rocking chair. She pointed her finger at me and the chair and warned, "Never rock an empty rocking chair, it means someone will die."

I was glad we didn't have a rocking chair at our house. She said the same thing would happen if I put a pair of shoes on top of a table. I told Mom about these strange things I had learned.

"Don't listen to her, superstitions are dangerous and untrue," Mom said.

When Ernie wasn't out running around in an old beat-up car, he helped his mother around the house and had a reputation as a good student and a trouble maker. He was also handsome, which was not lost on

Midway

my sister. She could sometimes be seen standing by the window of his car. After awhile, they started going places together.

Virgil brought home some chicks and dug a few rows of garden. He wanted to raise things like back on the farm. For Virgil, the farm was a piece of dry prairie near Fargo North Dakota. He spent his entire childhood there. I felt sorry for him. When he was a young boy he saw his mom collapse, carrying buckets of water to the barn, and die before his eyes. His dad was already dead. They were just children left alone on the family farm. His older sister, herself just a teen, took over and raised him and whatever siblings he had. He said his sister was an angry girl who mistreated him. A depression farm in North Dakota made Virgil eager for better times. In school he excelled at sports and loved baseball. During the war he served somewhere in the Pacific. He said he was a crane operator. He liked to say, "You can take the boy out of the country, but you can't take the country out of the boy." I understood the feeling.

I reconnected with my old friend Ronnie Olson. His Dad moved them to a triangle of land on Monster Road near Renton. Yes there really is a Monster Road. The triangle was defined by the Black River on one side and the Milwaukee and Union Pacific railroads on the short side, with the Duwamish River just beyond. The remaining side was bordered by a railroad siding and a gravel pit that made crushed rock. Between the Black River Bridge and the siding was just enough room for a narrow driveway leading to a small house, a tiny barn, a cow and some chickens. On the side nearest the railroad was an abandoned Union Pacific railroad building.

Mrs. Olson was going literally insane from the constant noise, but this triangle of trains was a kid's paradise. I spent two weeks in August with the Olson's and some additional weekends. On Sunday we went to the First Baptist church in Renton. On weekdays we went to Vacation Bible School. But, on Saturday we kids were allowed to walk to Renton for a matinee at the Roxy Theater.

We had plenty of time left over for other adventures; we picked wild blackberries and put them in bowls with sugar and milk, we read comic books in the old railroad house, we hid in the railroad trestle when trains crossed over the Black River, we watched trains go by and waved at the engineers, we built a raft and floated around on the Black River, we caught a 6-inch bullhead, then fried it by the riverside and ate it. We spent time on the river like Tom Sawyer and Huckleberry Finn, along with Ronnie's little brother who was always with us.

The only reason we had enough river to float around on was because the Duwamish River backed up into the Black River. The Black River was once a major river that flowed out of Lake Washington. The Duwamish Indians lived and fished where the Black River entered the Duwamish River, right here at the Olson's little farm. Early settlers used the Black River to boat goods from Lake Washington to Elliott Bay near Seattle. Now it was just a trickle, thanks to

Midway

engineers who rerouted Lake Washington through the Ballard Locks a hundred years earlier. This lowered the lake level so that no more water flowed out through the Black River.

There was no shortcut across the Duwamish River and we didn't dare take our raft across. To get to the little country store on the West Valley Highway meant walking along Monster Road past the Longacres horse track, over the railroads and the river bridge to the store. This was the closest place to buy candy, pop and comic books. Hobos, who were mostly homeless drunks, also shopped there. The store had a lot of cheap wine. This is probably where the money Ronnie's dad paid the hobos went. The hobos sold chickenfeed to Ronnie's dad that they swept from the floors of empty box cars.

Paul with Ronald Olson

The road was littered with racetrack paraphernalia. As we walked back past Longacres, Ronnie talked around a piece of red licorice, "I know where the hobos live. They're in the woods across from the farm."

"You been there?" I asked.

"No! Do you want to see it?"

"Sure," I answered.

We walked the rest of the way to the farm on Monster Road where it curled around a haystack-shaped hill with a small red house at the top. All around were fields with cattle and horses. It looked like English countryside. When we got back to the farm we didn't turn down the driveway. Instead, we followed the siding tracks away from the farm and into the woods, beside rows of boxcars. Big Leaf Maple, alder and other trees spread their limbs over the tracks, blocking out the midday sun and shading our path. We came to a pool of water fed by a length of pipe shoved into the hillside. A bar of soap sat on a large rock next to the pipe. Trails led from it into the surrounding trees. Ronnie looked up the largest trail that disappeared into the trees, and took a step forward.

"I'm scared," Charley said.

"Let's stay close together and see where the trail goes," I suggested.

Ronny continued on with Charley and me close behind.

"Hey, look at this," Ronny said, in a hushed voice.

Our eyes followed his. A hovel of scrap wood, cardboard and sticks sat away from the trail under a fir bow. Some clothes were spread out to dry on the bushes.

"Think anybody's home?" I whispered.

We crept farther up the trail. Well above the tracks was an open place in the woods. There stood a small house made of cardboard fastened to a stick frame. It was about six feet square with a roof shingled from flattened cans and other metal scraps. It had a door and a small window that was shuttered with

Midway

more cardboard.

Still whispering Ronnie said, "It even has a stove pipe."

"Did you see the flowerbed?" I added.

A row of rocks outlined some flowers and a clean path that led to the trail.

"Come on, let's see what else there is," I said, and we moved on.

We saw campsites and fire pits and a few more shelters, but nothing as nice as the square cardboard one. Then suddenly a hobo stepped into the path in front of us.

"Howdy, boys."

"Hello mister." One of us said in a tight voice.

"What are you boys doing here?"

"Nothin'."

"You boys better git before somethin' happens to ya."

"We were just leaving."

"You're the boys from the farm, aren't ya?"

"Yes sir."

"Don't come back."

"No sir, we won't."

We walked quickly and quietly down the trail past the first shelter. It wasn't just Charley who was afraid now. As soon as we saw the tracks, we ran the rest of the way out of the hobo jungle.

Back home, I hung around with Bob Adams from across the street, and got to know a few of his friends.

One of them was Lowell Ingberg, whose dad managed the Midway Drive-in Theater. The Ingbergs lived at the theater, or should I say *in* the theater. A several stories tall curved wooden building had a movie screen on one side, and a large "Midway Drive-in" sign on the other. In between was the Ingberg home. Their skinny apartment was only accessible through a single black door, under the screen, that opened into a storage room and a flight of wooden stairs. The door at the top opened into a skinny stack of rooms that was the Ingberg's claustrophobia-inducing home. The whole place had only two or three tiny windows that faced Puget Sound in the distance. The living room was sparsely furnished, but had a TV set. The living room also had a peephole in the wall, which went through the middle of the movie screen, so you could see the drive-in parking lot. A rope, hung three stories below the kitchen window, to a newspaper tube that was hoisted up every morning so they could retrieve the paper.

Because he lived at the drive-in, everyone knew Lowell, but not everyone liked him. He had a foul mouth and an unnatural eye for girls and women. He also hung around with Ernie Adams who was much older than him. But everyone liked his dad, he let neighborhood kids sit by the speaker posts and watch movies -- no charge.

I loved to spend nights at the drive-in. Even in rainy weather kids could be seen sitting under umbrellas and blankets by a bare speaker post. Kids usually sat in the back row next to the woods. The snack bar was half buried in the center of the parking lot. Sometimes on cold rainy nights, when there were

Midway

almost no customers, it was okay for us kids to stand in the snack bar and watch the movie through the front window.

Before the movie started, a game called Spotty was played on the screen. Many cars in the '50s had spotlights. They were especially fashionable on young men's cars, usually with one on each side. Teardrop baby spots were the best. The game was played when a little character called Spotty,

Paul and Bobby in a soap box racer

was projected onto the screen. The object was to try and hit Spotty with your spotlight before he moved somewhere else. Spotlights covered the screen. This activity also signaled the kids, playing on the rides bellow the screen, that the cartoons were about to start.

Another friend was Lawny Holly. He lived just south of the drive-in on Highway 99 where his parents had a gas station and garage. They lived in the back. The Holly's also had a television and I was invited to watch the Seafair unlimited hydroplane races at their house.

I met him on a hill behind the drive-in. Kids took their flimsy soapbox racers there for downhill racing. They didn't look much like racers, but they coasted down the hill fast enough. Lawny had a racer made of metal that his dad built for him. The rest of the boys made their own wooden ones. But they all had two things in common, a rope to pull them with and no brakes. Downhill racing came natural to kids who lived at the top of several downhill roads.

I tore my Radio Flier wagon apart and used the wheels and axles to build my own soapbox. I had plenty of tools in my green wooden toolbox. I built several designs; open, enclosed, long and short. Some had rear wheel steering, and some had all wheel steering, but most had a steering wheel that used ropes to turn the front axle. Other kids had weird designs too.

They were all dangerous. For example, across Highway 99 from the drive in was the mile long Zenith hill. Bob Adams had a soapbox that sat two kids with a large box on the front, which held the steering wheel. We pulled the racer to the top of the hill and got in. Soon we were moving along fast. We were leaning into the wind when Bob said, "The left front wheel is coming off."

I got on the wooden box hood and started kicking the wheel back on.

"Kick harder!" Bob yelled helplessly, from behind the steering wheel.

I kicked harder, but the wheel fell off anyway. The plank frame hit the pavement and the soapbox stopped dead still. I kept going, hitting the gravel in a sitting position, and flipping over into some blackberries. A planetarium of stars appeared inside my blackened head. Blackberry thorns stuck in my

Midway

skin. Bob bruised his chest.

Another incident was a racer using full sized bicycle wheels in the back, and tricycle wheels in front. It looked like a John Deer tractor. The designer and I sat next to each other on a flat board with our feet on a two-by-four. We pushed off down a long hill toward Des Moines. It was fast -- too fast. It started to sway then swerve, and then it fell completely apart as the wheels collapsed. Every board came loose and we skidded through the wreckage and rolled down the pavement. We got scratched and bruised but nothing worse.

The only lasting injury I received came when I fell off of a six passenger rolling platform called the Lumber Wagon. The full weight of five kids and the Lumber Wagon rolled over my wrist. My hand was useless for days. It took years before it felt normal again. Typically, I said nothing to my mother.

The Lumber Wagon was the floor of a small four-door sedan, without doors, that I made to park at the drive-in. It gave Bob, Lawny and me shelter from the rain, but fell apart when it tipped over on the way home, leaving just a platform. The way it crashed was unfortunate. We were running because of the rain. When we pulled the cart into Bob's driveway it flopped over and ripped apart. My dog was curled up on our blankets and came rolling out with the ripped loose boards. She stood in the rain and looked up at me with her big round eyes as if to say, "That hurt, but you're forgiven". I felt bad. All of my succeeding creations were short, narrow and light.

Sleeping out was popular too. Some parents let their kids sleep outside in the summer. Other parents knew better. We had two favorite places, a labyrinth of Scotch Broom across from the drive–in, and the woods behind the drive-in. We rolled up in quilts and pillows and slept like babies well into the morning. This was because we stayed up late into the night being delinquent. Typically we hung out at the drive-in, and then walked around Midway looking for excitement, like throwing a rock on somebody's roof or tossing firecrackers which, at that time, were illegal. Finally we sat in our bedding drinking Cokes, practicing grown-up language, telling dirty jokes and making up scary stories. They liked me to make up the stories.

I lowered my voice and started, "One day my friend Ronny and I snuck deep into the Black River hobo jungle and came face-to-face with a huge ugly bum. We ran for our lives but he kept coming, his long knife glistening in the sun. He couldn't keep up because he had a bad limp. Every time he put his foot down it squeaked, and he yelled, 'I'm going get you brats, just wait and see'. Late that night I heard the barn yard gate slam shut, then 'squeak' 'squeak'..." I improvised.

The summer was wearing on when Virgil's brother Jalmer and his friend, Doctor Barrett, arrived from Alaska where they had been working. The doctor did something impressive. He picked up my Boy Scout manual and gracefully wrote my name on the first page. My name flowed across the page with a bird in flight worked into the art. He was a gifted

Midway

calligrapher.

The Boy Scout manual didn't last long. My scout master playfully slapped me across the stomach, knocking the wind out of me. When I caught my breath I jumped up from the floor yelling and cursing as I ran to the door. I ripped my scout manual to shreds on the way out. Dr. Barrett's beautiful calligraphy lay in the mud. I never went back to the Boy Scouts.

The doctor left after a few days, but Jalmer stayed on to help Virgil with some home improvements. Jalmer quickly built a set of cupboards for the house. He then constructed a detached garage with a washroom for Mom and, at last, a bedroom for me. I both liked and admired Virgil's carpenter brother. I thought I might like to be a carpenter someday.

When the garage was finished, I moved into my new bedroom. It was lonely sleeping away from the house, but I had my dog Bobby to keep me company. At night, we lay curled up in our quilt falling asleep to the faraway sounds of foghorns on Puget Sound and trains in the Kent valley. Most trains had Diesel engines with horns that blasted their presence, but I listened for the few great steam engines that were still on the tracks.

At night when the land lay silent, the steam whistle's call drifted for miles to awaken the imagination of those who listened to its lonely cry. Its eerie tone had musical qualities that inspired thoughts of faraway places, freedom and adventure. Great music was penned from that soon to be forgotten sound, with words like, "Now the rain's a fallin', hear the train a callin' … ol' clickety clack's a echoin' back, the blues in the night"

Chapter 15

Last Trip Home

Jalmer was heading home to North Dakota. Since Virgil had a new car, he and Mom decided to take a trip to Minnesota and drop Jalmer off on the way. Virgil and Jalmer also had a niece who wanted go home to North Dakota. We would pick up her and her little baby in Portland. We left on Labor Day weekend.

From Portland, we headed across Eastern Washington to Highway 10 for our journey to Minnesota. Our car was full. Virgil, Mom and I sat in front. Jalmer, the niece and the baby sat in back. It was hot and nobody knew what an air conditioned car was. We just rolled the windows down. Up ahead of us was an impressively large dust devil spinning its way across the desert. "Whoosh", the wind hit our car. The inside filled with dust and it was gone. We pulled into Missoula Montana after dark. The only room we could find was in a really ugly old hotel. We were hot, dirty and sweaty. The only bathroom was down the hall. So we had to take turns using it. Mom asked me to watch the baby while its mother went to the shower.

"Okay," I said, apprehensively. Everyone left the room and the baby lay on the bed. Before I knew it, the baby had rolled to the edge of the bed. As soon as it fell on the floor it began to scream. I didn't know what to do. I was standing looking at it when its mother rushed into the room and rescued the baby.

Mom yelled at me. "I told you to watch the baby.

Why weren't you watching her?

"I was watching! It rolled off the bed!"

"You could have stopped her," Mom barked.

"I didn't know it could roll."

"I guess you can't be trusted around the baby," she said.

That was fine with me. I was afraid of the thing anyway and wanted nothing to do with it.

As we crossed Montana the next day, a motorcycle fell in behind us. It wanted to pass but hadn't had a chance yet. In the back seat, the baby was crying. The niece changed its messy diaper. It was a paper one that could be thrown away. Since there were no littering laws to worry about, she threw it out the window. I watched it catch the wind and come open, then hit the motorcyclist. He wiped it away and whipped his motorcycle off the road where he disappeared from view.

"Mom, Mom, did you see that? She threw a diaper out the window, and it hit a guy on a motorcycle?"

"No it didn't," Mom said sternly.

"It did too, I saw it hit him in the face," I said

"That's enough," she snapped.

The baby was still crying and Virgil started driving a lot faster. I stuck my little plastic airplane out the window and watched the propellers spin in the wind.

The next day we were in North Dakota stalled in traffic, waiting for construction delays. We finally got to Fargo where Virgil had a sister.

Last Trip Home

We went to see Virgil's boyhood home and visited relatives, then left in some relatives new Nash Ambassador that everyone called an upside down bath tub. Jalmer was still with us but his niece and her screaming baby had reached their destination.

Finally we arrived at Grandma Strand's house where I was left to spend precious time with Grandma and my cousin Sharon, while Mom, Virgil, Jalmer and the owner of the bathtub shaped car went off on their own. After they left, Sharon and I ran along behind them for a while then walked along the road following their tire tracks. Then we saw a fresh moose print on the tire tracks, and then we saw a bear print on the tire track. In the few minutes that had passed since the car left, these dangerous animals were on the road. Just as we approached a place where the water crossed the road, the bushes on one side of the road shook. We froze and stared at the bushes, then the bushes on the other side of the road shock. We turned tail and ran as fast as we could for the farm. We cut across the field and climbed a haystack. We looked back for the first time. Nothing had followed us. We slid down and returned to the house.

Like all farm kids, Sharon and I climbed the ladder in the barn and jumped down into the hay. We looked at old stereoscope pictures that were in the barn, played games on the stair landing in the house, and hung around with Grandma. In a couple of days, Mom and Virgil came back. This time they were in Virgil's car. Soon I said good-bye to Sharon and then to my Grandma Strand, who I would never see again.

When Grandpa Was a Kid

Next stop was the Landgren farm, where Grandpa was busy killing potato bugs. I helped him for a while. The bugs were almost a half-inch long with black and yellow stripes. Once a bucket of bugs was gathered he threw them into a flaming fifty-five-gallon burn barrel where they snapped and popped as they were incinerated.

Grandpa suddenly had to go into the little town of Cloquet and motioned for me to come along. I hopped into his green Studebaker pickup and we took off. On the way back, he stopped at the Big Lake tavern, the same place where the rooster chased me when I was a toddler. In Washington State no kids are allowed in taverns, but it was okay here in Minnesota, so I sat up to the bar like a real man and drank pop. I noticed some little plastic telescopes hanging on the wall behind the bar.

"Hey Grandpa, do you think I could have one of those telescopes?" I asked.

"Are you sure that's what you want?" Grandpa asked.

"yeah," I said.

"What are you going to do with it?"

"Look through it."

"Okay!" Grandpa ordered the telescope, looked through it for awhile, and handed it to me. I held it up my eye and to my surprise, it wasn't a telescope at all. It contained a picture of a naked woman. With a great deal of embarrassment, I shoved it in my pocket.

When our visit came to an end and it was time to leave for home, Grandma Landgren came to the car window and handed me a piece of Grandpa's hardtack with a thick layer of her sour cream butter. She knew how much I loved her butter. I would see this grandma again.

When Grandpa Was a Kid

Chapter 16

The Wrong School

We got home two weeks after school started. Like most summers, it ended with me going to a new school. I had my choice of schools to enroll in. Midway wasn't only midway between cities it was also midway between two school districts. We lived in the Highline school district, but the Federal Way School District started just across the street. Since Bob, Lowell and some other kids I met that summer went to Federal Way, I walked to their bus stop and started junior high at Federal Way. This was a choice I would regret for years to come. Such a decision should not have been left up to me. I should have gone to Highline. Maybe things would have turned out better.

The bus driver picked us up at the most northerly bus stop in the district, and drove us to school on highway 99. We made a few stops, and then pulled up into to the school parking lot.

The school was long, with a grade school on one end, junior high in the middle, and high school at the other end. Each year students moved farther down the hall until they finally graduated. As usual, I had a window seat. Outside were sidewalks, a couple of small buildings, an athletic field and the forest beyond. There was a lot of between-class traffic outside my window. Once, two high school girls got into a catfight right in front of my window. They pulled hair, scratched at each other and ripped clothes, all the while, screaming and cursing. Bullying and fighting were more common at this school than in any school I had yet attended. I soon experienced it first hand on the playground and would learn to adjust to it.

Paul age 13, by the garage that Jalmer built

The community of Federal Way had just a few buildings along the sides of Highway 99. As they say, "If you blink you'll miss it." The school was the biggest building. There were also some small white wooden stores, a gas station and a feed store. A few houses were scattered around. Most kids were bused in from the surrounding countryside, places like Star Lake, Steel Lake, Redondo, Dash Point, and places that didn't have names.

I didn't like this school. For one thing they had organized PE with a football field, track and gymnasium. They required special clothing, which I never had. Worst of all, they had showers. Every day after PE we had to take off our clothes and run naked into the showers, along with the whole boys class. This was all new to me and I didn't want anything to do with it.

"Why aren't you suited up?" I was repeatedly asked.

The Wrong School

"I don't have anything to wear." I never bothered to ask for athletic clothes at home. The coach found some cast offs and I wore those. I never brought them home to be cleaned.

One day after PE I was running my pathetic body around the corner to the shower room when a not so pathetic, athletic boy came around the corner the other way. We hit head on. I flipped flat on my back in pain, squirming around naked on the cold wet floor while other students laughed their guts out. A bunch of pale white naked boys with no self respect at all. I spent the rest of the day in the nurse's office.

I hated school and was always impatient to leave. The clock on the wall advanced in one-minute jerks. I stared at the clock until it hit 3:15, then left with the bell, for my bus. But the ride home had its own problems. Our evening bus driver was Deputy Sheriff Simms. I sat at the back of the bus and sometimes the other kids would push me around. They tried to get me mad enough to fight back or swear at them. Once, when my head hit and cracked a window, I started cursing my antagonists with all I had. I yelled loud enough to attract the bus driver's attention, but Deputy Simms didn't seem to care what happened on his bus.

That changed one day, when somebody dangled a black rubber spider in front of one of the nice girls in the front seat. She was also one of our few black students. She screamed, "eeeeek, get it away, get it away!"

The bus abruptly stopped and great big Deputy Simms was out of his seat in a flash. He reached out and grabbed the perpetrator. "You can't do that on my bus. Get off!"

"I can't. How will I get home?"

The door swung open and the guilty kid was pushed off. The now quiet bus resumed its route.

Staying home sick was always a good way to skip school, but I made a mistake when I stayed home complaining about a toothache. Oral hygiene wasn't anything I practiced. I never brushed my teeth and no one told me to. I remember my dad saying. "I never brush my teeth, chewing snuff prevents cavities." As soon as Virgil found out I had a cavity, I was on my way to the dentist.

The dentist's office was in downtown Seattle. Looking up from the sidewalk, I saw windows with, "Painless Dentist" painted on them.

Mom got off the elevator first and we walked into a small waiting room. We sat down to wait. "Aaaaah" came a muffled scream.

"Mom," I whispered, "Are you sure this is going to be painless."

"Don't worry," she assured me.

"Aaaaah," Another scream came from the depth of the dentist's office.

I remembered Grandma Strand telling me about how her teeth were extracted by a visiting dentist who came to the farm. She sat in a kitchen chair. The dentist pulled a tooth and Grandma jumped out the chair and ran around the kitchen crying out. When the pain subsided she sat down and did it again.

A door opened and an old white haired dentist

The Wrong School

stepped out. "Paul?"

I followed him to his operatory. I sat with my mouth open. He immediately grabbed his drill and started drilling into a tooth. The drill vibrated my head. Then came the stabbing pain. I whimpered and pulled hard on the armrests. Tears flowed down my cheeks. Then he attacked another tooth. I told myself, *don't scream*. I didn't want mom to hear me. He kept giving me some pink liquid to rinse my mouth. I spit out bloody pink liquid and chunks of my own teeth. When the drilling ended he pounded silver amalgam into the holes. Then he resumed grinding. I would have confessed to murder if he would stop – his murder. Smoke rose from my mouth as he cut into my gums and nicked my cheek. I finally rinsed out more blood and chunks of silver. He was done. He missed the cavity I originally complained about.

Back in the waiting room, Mom said. "That wasn't so bad, was it?"

I kept my throbbing mouth shut.

Nights and weekends were free from school, and didn't include homework. I never did home work. Virgil had been a good student and wanted to introduce homework into my life. He probably could have, but I started complaining, "I don't understand." Which was true, but I preferred to avoid school.

Mom joined in with, "I had trouble in school too. Don't force him, after all you're only a kid once".

"He'll fail if he doesn't do something about his homework."

This degenerated into another serious argument

between Mom and Virgil, leaving me free of homework. Eventually Virgil gave up, but I was the real loser.

Chapter 17

The Logging Accident

One evening, Zola came to the house to tell us that my dad had broken his back in a logging accident. Since we didn't have a phone, the message came to the Adams house, from the hospital in Centralia. I remembered the time Dad told me about the injured logger he took to the same hospital on the back of his truck. Now it had happened to him. Virgil loaned his car to Floyd Adams who drove Mom, Mavis and me on our mission. We left under a grey winter sky to rescue my dad.

When we got to the hospital we learned he had been discharged the night before. We got his address from the hospital and headed for Riffe, a tiny logging community in the Cascade foothills near Mount St Helens. We found out he took a bus as far as he could, then walked the rest of the way home. Floyd stopped and talked to somebody who told us they saw a crippled man walking along the road. We followed the road to where he was staying. We pulled into a yard with a house, outbuildings and some logging equipment. Floyd asked at the house. I saw a man point to a tent. Mavis went to the tent and peeked around the flap.

"Oh, Mavis I'm so glad to see you!" he said.

He was lying on a small cot next to a small wood burning cook stove that kept his little home warm. The tent had a wooden floor and short wooden sides. The whole thing couldn't have been bigger than eight by ten feet. He was plenty happy to see us. He struggled to sit up. We helped gather some of his belongings and got him in the car.

On the way home he explained his accident.

"My back and neck are broken," he began. "I was standing on a log several feet above the ground, tossing another log up onto a pile, and then the bark popped off of the log I was standing on. I flipped backward toward the ground. My lower back struck another log and I could feel the bones break. At the same time, the log I was holding came down on my neck."

Clifford Strand
before the accident

He explained that some other loggers pulled him out and got him into the back of a pick-up truck and to the hospital in Centralia.

"They gave me pain medicine and put me in traction."

Then somebody asked, "Why did they let you out of the hospital?"

"They couldn't do anything more for me. I was told to go home and rest," he said.

The ride home was hard on him. I can't remember where we took him, but I know he twice spent several months in the Swedish Hospital in Seattle in body casts, after having spinal fusions on his lumbar and

The Logging Accident

cervical spine.

This life changing accident left him crippled and in pain for the rest of his eighty-three years. For years afterword I heard the tragic story repeated, and always with the admonition of, "Never work in the woods."

When Grandpa Was a Kid

Chapter 18

Television and Mortality

I usually had a little money of my own. I sold pop bottles, delivered papers for paperboys who needed a day off, sold an occasional fixed up bike, did a little work for a local nursery, and saved much of whatever allowance money I was given.

Most of my money was spent on movies, comic books, food, and models from the hobby shop. I liked to roll my money so that the ones were in the middle and a five or ten showed on the outside. I also kept a fat coin purse.

Somehow, Mom got indebted to me for several dollars. This worked to my benefit. I went along to an auction where Mom and Virgil were looking for a piece of furniture. Suddenly the auctioneer presented a television set. It was low, wide and black with a small round screen on one side of the flat front. A panel of knobs filled the rest of the space. It looked like it was pulled out of an electronics laboratory. I wanted it.

"Bid on it Mom," I said, enthusiastically.

"We don't need it."

I argued my case. "Buy this TV, and I'll forget your loan."

Mom turned to Virgil, "What do you think?"

Virgil raised his hand. We were bidding. Soon I heard "sold", and the auctioneer's finger was pointing at us.

When Grandpa Was a Kid

At the time, TVs were uncommon curiosities that people stood and watched in showroom windows. The only families I knew that had one were the Engbergs with their 17" Silvertone, and whatever Lawny Holly's family had. I was probably the only 13 year old kid with his own TV.

At home, I placed the TV on a chair and started figuring out how to make it work. The screen was nine inches across and perfectly round. I recognized the on/off knob and the channel tuner. I turned it on and waited for it to warm up. It hissed and presented a snowy screen. It needed an antenna.

I took apart an electric train transformer and unwound the thin wire, then threw two lengths of wire over the roof of the house and screwed the ends to the back of the TV. With that, all three channels could be found. The rest was a mystery. Rows of knobs were labeled; vertical hold, horizontal hold, bright, contrast, height, width, focus and some more that twisted the picture or made waves. The knobs on the back did more dramatic adjustments. The picture was a mess. I kept turning knobs until eventually, everything was adjusted.

"Hey, Mavis, it works!"

Mavis stuck her head around the corner. "Oh. Let me see," she said.

We changed channels to see what was on. Every so often, more adjustments were needed to hold the picture steady. But it worked, and we sat back and watched TV. That night we had our first family TV night.

Television and Mortality

On a Saturday afternoon, while Mom was working at Betty's Cafe, Mavis and Ernie sat close together on the couch watching useless daytime shows on my pathetic little TV.

I started teasing them, "Hey why are you sitting so close? Are you in love?"

Mavis asked me to leave them alone.

"I don't have to, it's my TV."

I crawled up on the back of the couch and asked some more stupid questions.

Ernie had had enough. "Get out of here!" he yelled, and gave me a push.

My wad of gum sliped down the wrong pipe, and I began to choke. I gagged and bent over, running around the room turning color. The two lovebirds were on their feet.

"Do something," Mavis yelled.

I felt like I was blacking out and thought; *Ernie killed me!* Then the gum shot clear of my mouth and I gasped for air. I looked at my presumed killer and grabbed a flowerpot, "you son-of-a-bitch."

I hurled the pot at Ernie's head. He ducked.

I grabbed another pot, "you bastard."

The pot just missed his head and smashed against the piano.

"I'm going to kill you!"

More pots flew and still Ernie didn't get hit. Mom had lots of potted plants and most of them narrowly missed lover boy's terrorized skull.

Before I reached the last pot, my anger was spent.

Mavis pragmatically said, "We better clean this

up, Mom will be off work in a few minutes."

Ernie and I exchanged apologies and began cleaning. Miraculously, only two or three pots broke, and we found replacements.

Just as I was sweeping up the last of the dirt, Mom walked in. She greeted us with a cheerful. "Hi! What are you doing, Paul?"

"I spilled a plant."

"Which one was it?"

"The prayer plant."

Ernie went home. I now had the TV to myself

Chapter 19

Learning to Smoke

The last day of school finally arrived and Virgil was right, I would fail if I didn't do my homework. At the end of the last day of seventh grade, after our little party was over and report cards were about to be handed out, my teacher led me into the hall and told me I had failed the seventh grade.

"Think of this as an opportunity to do better next year," he said. Then he added, "You should consider summer school."

He waited while I dried my eyes, then we went in to the classroom.

The ride home was embarrassing. Everyone on the bus knew I flunked. They were all looking at me to see what a failure looked like. Now I had to tell my mom and be sent off to summer school, while everyone else was having fun. I walked in the house. Mom was home.

"Here's my report card." I put the incriminating evidence in her hand, and said, "I flunked."

I waited until she read the report, and then I asked, "Do I have to go to summer school?"

"Don't worry," she said, "You have only one childhood. Forget about it and enjoy your summer."

That was that. I was going to be in the same grade next year. I felt very unimportant, *maybe I am retarded*, I thought, *maybe that's why I never understand what's going on*.

When Grandpa Was a Kid

I went out in search of other kids. There was a sleep-out planned.

That summer I met a boy my age named Jim McCann, who lived over on Military Road. A quarter mile path through the forest connected my street to his. At the other end of the path the woods opened into the large backyard of a man who didn't care if kids used his yard for a short cut. He had several little garden houses scattered around his copious back yard. They were made of sticks and tarpaper and painted fancy colors. On the inside were bars and little tables with dirt floors. The walls were hung with magazine pictures of scantily dressed women. The whole yard was designed for drinking and partying. Jim and I explored it on our trips back and forth to Midway.

One night we walked right through a party in progress. Lights were strung up, music flowed and the aroma of grilled meat filled the air. Happy black men and women were enjoying a warm summer evening. I spent that night with Jim sleeping on his lawn. We laid awake on that warm clear night identifying planets and stars.

The next day we cut back through the trail, and were walking along Highway 99 when Jim reached down and grabbed a cigarette package.

"Look at this," he said. "There's a cigarette in here."

Later that day we hid in Jim's backyard fort to try the cigarette. It was a Kool. Jim lit it. We passed it back and forth sucking in its harsh thick smoke.

"You ever smoke one of these before?" I asked.

Learning to Smoke

"Sure, I took one of my dad's. Have you?"

"Yeah, at the drive-in," I answered. "Have you ever inhaled?"

"No."

"One of the guys at the drive-in said all you had to do was fill your mouth with smoke and breathe in.", I shared.

Jim tried it. He immediately began choking and coughing. I took the cigarette. After watching Jim's response, I decided to take only a little smoke. I breathed it in. It burned all the way down. I began to choke and gag. Tears ran down our cheeks. I stared back at the equally distressed Jim and was suddenly dizzy. We finished the cigarette. All the rest of the day my lungs hurt.

There was something attractive about smoke. Even though the experience was bad, we both wanted to try it again. I stole a couple of Lucky Strikes from Virgil's unattended pack.

The second time we tried smoking was just as bad as the first time, but we learned that inhaling could be done. We lit up and began smoking a whole cigarette each.

"I think I'm going to be sick," Jim said, as he snubbed out his cigarette in the dirt.

"I don't feel good either," I answered, while rubbing a sore, watery eye that got filled with raw smoke.

I went home dizzy and sick. My lungs hurt more than before.

Still attracted to tobacco, we eventually discovered

that with practice the smoke went down easily and the dizziness felt good. Then came the nagging desire for more. We continued our exploration of tobacco. We smoked pipes, cigars, roll-your-owns and chewed plug. All of it was terrible, especially a corncob pipe with Bull Durham that smoked hot and strong and kept going out. But even worse was the Copenhagen snuff, like my dad chewed. After a few days we forgot about tobacco except for an occasional cigarette, which had become culturally important around other kids. Eventually I owned my own pack that I kept hidden behind the house. I took it with me when I went places without adults.

Chapter 20

Outlaws and In-laws

The summer soon filled with excitement. Ernie had an old beat up car and took Bob and me, and sometimes Lowell, swimming. There were plenty of places to swim. At Star Lake there was a dock to jump from, and I knew a couple of kids from school who lived there. One was Gary, who had a horse. One day he kicked the animal with his heals to make it go, but instead it let a long loud horse sized fart. After that, any time Gary was seen on his horse kids would yell, "hey Gary, make it fart."

Steel Lake was a little farther away but had a better beach so we went there, too.

Lake Fenwick was small and surrounded by hills and thick woods. The lake had old logs floating around in it and snags sticking up. It had a nice little park with a roped off beach, but the water was dark.

I may have saved Lowell's life when he went beyond the ropes and got stuck in the lily pads. I was a poor swimmer and was dog-paddling around in an inner tube, when I saw Lowell struggling to get free of the lilies and gasping for air. I grabbed the rope at the edge of the swimming area and threw my tube as hard as could in his direction. He reached out and grabbed it and was safe. I bravely dog paddled back to shore. The Adams brothers were out in the middle of the lake swimming among the snags.

On the other side of Kent valley was Lake

Meridian. It was a large lake and had a large beach with several diving boards. There were also rental boats. We rented two pedal boats and went out onto the lake and had a firecracker fight. Lowell burned his fingers when he held his arm back too long before the toss.

The best place to go was the Angle Lake Plunge, not far from SeaTac Airport. They had everything; a tall water slide, a swing, diving boards, a long dock, and a big raft. But best of all, it had a wide sand beach with lots of kids. After swimming we put our trunks on the antenna and drove around the countryside while they dried.

Ernie kept company with kids years younger than himself. He drove around with them late at night stealing things out of cars. I know this from firsthand experience. Late one night we pulled up beside a car with our lights turned off. Ernie sneaked out and lifted the parked car's trunk lid, and pulled out a toolbox that he transferred to his own trunk. He got back in the car and let the clutch out. The wheels began to spin. We were stuck. When Ernie and another kid got out to push, the porch light came on. A man came to our car "What's going on?" he asked. I was petrified with fear imagining cops and handcuffs. *Oh, God please help us get away*

"I'm stuck," Ernie replied.

"Let me see if I can help," the man offered.

He went and got his car and put its front bumper against Ernie's back bumper and pushed until Ernie's car was free. We were off.

"Thanks," Ernie yelled from his window.

"You're welcome," replied the victim.

I couldn't stand it. I was in the car with a real criminal. I watched out the back window as the man happily waved to us. I felt scared and guilty.

Late on another night Ernie, Bob, Lowell, one or two other kids and I drove to Kent. Ernie got the audacious idea to tease the Kent police. He drove up to the curb on the wrong side of the street in front of the police station. He left the car running and sprinted up the few steps to the front door, stuck his cigarette on the fuse of a firecracker, opened the door, and tossed it in. He ran back to his car and took off. Cops came running out like wasps from a nest. Ernie turned on to Meeker Street and was out of town before the cops had a chance to catch him. Going places with Ernie became criminal, but I couldn't seem to avoid him.

Mavis' relationship with Ernie eventually brought her to announce that she intended to marry him. She was pregnant, and wanted to do the right thing and establish a home with Ernie and their future child. I overheard bits and pieces of various conversations.

"But why?" Mom asked in a desperate voice, "He's three years younger than you."

"I love him."

"It won't work. You can't marry him."

"Mom, you don't understand. I have to be married. Besides, he wants to marry me."

Everyone knew that Ernie was immature. If Mavis knew, she overlooked it. Ernie was the guy who provided neighborhood kids with pictures of naked women from a nudist magazine. I had one of them hidden along with my cigarettes.

"Please consider what you're doing. What kind of life can he offer you?" Mom pleaded.

Virgil implored Mavis not to get married. "We can take the baby and raise it as our own. Just don't marry that boy."

Mavis persisted and a wedding was scheduled for July. The ceremony was at the Adam's house, in their front yard. The bride and groom were suited up and looked beautiful and handsome. Zola saw to it that there was plenty of good food.

Mavis and Earnest Adams on their wedding day

The couple rented a small upstairs apartment in an old house in Kent. Mavis had it decorated and ready to start a family, but she spent her wedding night alone. Her new husband disappeared after the wedding party, and didn't show up until the next day. Needless to say, Mavis was crushed.

Mom counseled her. "You can get it annulled." But, Mavis loved this man and would stick with him.

My dad bought the new couple a sleek two-tone green 1948 Hudson Hornet coupe. It had "Ernie" painted on the driver's door just under the window and "Mavis" written on the other. Ernie drove that car over one hundred miles an hour through the farm country on the west valley Highway. Before long he wrecked it. My dad then bought him a 1940 Buick. That too was soon ruined. They moved when the rent was overdue.

When Grandpa Was a Kid

Chapter 21

Snipe Hunting at the Drive-in Theater

Occasionally I saw Ronny. We did some of the things we did last summer, like church and rafting. Charley was proud of himself for rafting out into the Duwamish River and back. We begged him never to do that again. We also went to a carnival in Burien. We went on the most exiting ride of our lives, the Octopus. We got on and started twirling and dipping as the big black machine swung us around. All at once, the front panel fell open. By the grace of God, we were not holding on to its handholds, because they fell with it, along with our seat belts. We both had our arms over the back and hung onto it, feet dangling out the open front. The operator stopped the ride before we were flung to the ground. We didn't even get our money back.

On a sunny Saturday morning in Seattle, Mom took me up the escalators of the Bon Marche to the toy floor. She was going to buy me a new bike. When we got there, rows of Schwinn Corvettes and Corvelles, in beautiful two-tone colors, greeted us. But there were several other kinds of bikes too.

Mom said, "Which one do you like?"

"I don't know," I said.

We looked at them all. Then my eyes settled on a plain black one. It was an English bike called an Indian Scout. It had a Sturmey-Archer three-speed rear end, a narrow leather seat and a package rack on the back. It was the only one of its kind in the store.

"I like this one, Mom."

She looked at it like there was something wrong with it.

"Are you sure? It looks kind of flimsy."

"Yes, I'm sure. I want this one," I insisted.

"Wouldn't you rather have a Schwinn? They sure are pretty"

"No, they're not good bikes. They have bad brakes."

I noticed the Indian Scout had two wheel hand brakes.

"Besides," I added, "The Scout hardly costs anymore."

Mom smiled happily and bought the bike.

I rode it everywhere. It could travel up hills without having to get off and push.

After a few days, I decided to go see Ronny, while Mom and Virgil were at work. I packed the barest essentials in a suitcase, filled it the rest of the way with comic books, fastened it to the rear rack and took off. I peddled my way along Highway 99 to Riverton Heights, then down to the valley and on to Ronny's place – about fifteen miles.

When I turned into the Olson's driveway Ronny and Charley were out in the pasture. They were surprised to see me. Mrs. Olson was surprised too, but not at all happy. She hadn't expected me. Then she saw all my comic books and warned that nothing but trouble could come from those comics. That evening she called my mom. To my surprise I could stay a few

Snipe Hunting at the Drive-in Theater

days. On Saturday, we walked to the Roxy Theater in Renton, and spent the day having fun together. But that night I slept alone in the old railroad house. It was spooky. It didn't even have a door and I worried about hobos and other imagined dangers, even insects. Ronnie and Charley had slept there a few days earlier, and when Charley got up the next morning there were yellow jackets in his pants that stung him repeatedly. He ran to the house without his pants.

All night, trains shook the little house as they rumbled passed and faded into the distance leaving a silence that magnified my imagination. I dreamed I was floating helplessly from my bunk toward the open door, while blood dripped from my nose. I awoke with a start. The sun was just rising. I saw dry blood on my pillow and there was more on my face. I had a bloody nose. Then I glanced at the floor. There was a trail of blood all the way to door, just as though I had really floated there. I jumped out of bed and pulled on my pants, with a quick check for yellow jackets. Although the blood stopped at the door, I didn't.

Mrs. Olson's predictions came true Sunday afternoon we began fighting over the comic books. Some other comics got mixed with mine and accusations flew as we tried to claim our rightful literature. That evening Virgil's maroon Chevy came down the driveway. It was time for me to go.

On one of the last warm summer nights, four of us hung around the back row of the Midway Drive-in watching the same movie we saw the night before. Bob broke the boredom with a story about how Indians use to go night hunting for birds called snipes. It was simple. They built a bonfire. Some of them went into the woods to scare out snipes, while others danced around the fire carrying large bags and making loud war whoops. Scared from their nests, the birds fled toward the light of the fire but the war whoops scared them, so they flew into the bags to hide. The Indian pulled the bag shut and the bird was caught.

Bob ended his story saying, "I've done this and it works."

"So have I", said Lowell. "Let's do it."

We went into the woods behind the drive-in to collect firewood while Lowell ran off to the storeroom under the screen to find a bag. He came back with a big gunny sack just as we were getting the fire ready.

It was decided that Gary and I would get to catch the birds. Gary was a mildly retarded boy who lived in the trailer park next to our house, and loved to hang around the drive-in. I would hold the bag because snipes are large and can cause harm if the bag isn't shut immediately after they enter. We didn't want Gary to get hurt.

When the fire was blazing, the two seasoned hunters headed for the woods to scare snipes toward our fire. There was one last instruction. "Don't make any noise until we are out of sight."

As soon as they were gone Gary and I danced and jumped around the fire making the sounds we often heard in western movies. Our long shadows exaggerated our size. The firelight shined on the white paint of the back fence and the leaves of the trees

Snipe Hunting at the Drive-in Theater

beyond, as we strained our eyes in that direction for an incoming snipe.

Then we heard feet running towards us in the gravel. "Hey! What do you think you're doing?" It was a parking attendant in white coveralls.

"We're snipe hunting." Gary said, and began explaining.

"You idiots! There's no such thing as snipe hunting. Put that fire out and get out of here."

A few people had gotten out of their cars to see what was going on. Some of them were laughing at us. I could also hear familiar laughter coming from the woods.

When Grandpa Was a Kid

Chapter 22

Bad Company

School started as a rerun of the seventh grade, but this time I sat on the other side of the school building facing Highway 99 with a different teacher. She put me in the back row away from any hope of staring out the window. I began to pay attention to my studies. Not because I flunked, but because they were interesting. I still didn't do any homework.

Sometimes Lowell and I hitchhiked home from school. Occasionally we skipped school and hitchhiked to Tacoma to walk the streets and just mess around. On one trip we got into a conversation about growing up. We all knew from our parents that smoking would stunt our growth. Lowell and I, and some other kid, were standing by the side of the road with our thumbs out trying to hitch a ride and smoking cigarettes when Lowell said, "So what if smoking stunts your growth, I'm tall enough to be a man."

I had just been to the doctor and knew that I weighed one hundred thirteen pounds.

"Right," I said, "Who cares? We probably won't stop growing all at once anyway."

"I'm plenty big, I got into a fight in White Center and beat up a grown man," Lowell boasted.

Lowell's other friend picked up the idea. "I bet I could too. Why don't we find somebody and pick a fight?"

"Let's go to Pacific Avenue. Bums hang around

there. We could pick a fight and beat one up," Lowell suggested.

They were both looking at me waiting to see what I had to say.

"This is a school day, we could get in trouble."

I wanted nothing to do with fighting. The other two looked at me like I was some kind of idiot. A car stopped and the bravado ended. We were on our way to Tacoma.

All we did was walk around town. Lowell stole a quart of milk off of a porch and I spent the rest of the day feeling guilty about it. That afternoon we caught a Greyhound bus back to Midway. Now I had to forge a note about missing school.

I noticed a skinny red headed kid around Betty's Café. He introduced himself as Dick Miller. His mom worked mornings for Betty. They lived in the tiny apartment upstairs. He was in the same grade as me, but went to school in the Highline district. His Mom was seldom home at night, leaving Dick to do whatever he wanted. His dad lived in some other state. They had a decent television. Some times after school we watched TV at his apartment. Even though he practically lived in our backyard, Mom didn't want me to go there at night. She didn't like Dick's mother and told me to stay away from there.

One weekend I went to see Ronny and he showed me a cache of old military ammunition. There was lots of it. He and Charley found it along Monster Road in the woods near Empire Way, just a short walk from the Olson farm. The way they found it was Ronny and

Charley were horsing around and Charley wound up rolling down the hill by the road and right into the ammo. Ronny gave me some. I took it home and showed it around. Dick Miller wanted some, so I gave him two or three different kinds. A few days later I was called to the principal's office. Waiting for me were two deputy Sheriffs.

"Did you give Richard Miller any ammunition?" One asked.

"yes."

"How much?

"Three."

Where did you get the ammunition?"

I explained how.

"Do you have any guns?'

"Just a Red Ryder BB gun."

"What were you going to do with the ammunition?"

The questions went on and on. They asked about things I didn't even know about. I halfway expected them to ask me if I knew who stole the milk off so-and-so's porch in Tacoma. We finally got into their car and went to my house. They took the few rounds of ammunition I had. Then we went and got Ronny out of school so his ammunition could be collected. Ronny led the Deputy to the abandoned ammunition beside Monster Road. We stood and watched as the deputies gathered a bucketful of old military ammunition. They acted like this was a major crime shakedown worthy of a TV Dragnet episode. The Sheriff's department managed to pull three kids out of three different schools, lecture us, warn us and explain the whole thing to our parents, all over an abandoned bucket of bullets, and Dick Miller's stupid idea to take them to school.

This wasn't the last trouble Dick got me into. One rainy night, as we walked to the drive-in, Dick asked me to wait by the road while he looked inside of an abandoned log cabin. "Okay," I said, and he disappeared in the direction of the cabin. He came back and told me there were things in the cabin. He handed me some envelopes and asked if I wanted the stamps on them for my collection. They were old but common stamps and I didn't want them. We continued on our way.

Not many days later I was called into the principal's office again. This time I was accused of being an accomplice in a burglary.

"Do you know Richard Miller?" They knew I did.

"Yes."

"Did you help him burglarize a house?" They made it sound like a crime had been committed.

"No."

"That's not what Miller said," the Deputy firmly stated.

"What did he say?" I asked with true curiosity.

"He said you were his lookout while he robbed the house."

"There was no house. It was an old log cabin."

"So you were his lookout?" The deputy grinned.

"No I wasn't. I didn't do anything wrong."

Then one of them held a gold watch and chain in

front of me. "You ever see this before?'

"No. I want to know what's going on," I insisted.

"You know what's going on. Why don't you tell us?"

I explained what little I knew, but they weren't at all satisfied. Eventually they told me their side of the story. The Mayor of Kent was in a jewelry store on Meeker Street when Dick came in and tried to sell a gold watch. The Mayor thought Dick was trying to sell stolen property and called the police. Dick told the police he stole the watch out the cabin. When asked if anyone else was involved, he named me.

"I didn't know he was going to steal stuff!" I said. "I just stood by the road and waited for him."

"That makes you an accomplice," one of them said.

These deputies weren't going to give up. They associated me with the crime of having some ammunition, and my partner Dick's involvement in that.

"What other crimes have you committed?"

I couldn't stand it any longer. These lying cops had turned me into a criminal. They didn't believe a word I said, so I said no more. I prayed to God to get me out of this mess.

God did. The cops warned me profusely, then gathered their notes and left. They later met with my Mom and that was the end of it. Dick went to live in a foster home. I should have listened to Mom

The next bit of trouble came from an evil collie that hated kids. It belonged to a woman who managed a rent-by-the-month motel just a few blocks from our house. She too hated kids.

I was helping a friend deliver newspapers. As we passed the motel the collie came out of nowhere and ripped open my pants, leaving my leg with contusions and abrasions. I showed Mom and Virgil my swollen, red leg. They called the Sheriff. The deputy told me to stop harassing the dog. The deputy probably recognized me as the neighborhood criminal and wouldn't believe my story.

Soon after this incident my boss at my part time job at the Midway Nursery sent me on a delivery. I was given an armload of plants and dispatched to the motel where the collie lived. When I got there, the evil dog ran right up to me and bit my fingers. The owner called it back. I didn't even get a tip. That was more than I could tolerate.

I took a broken hunting knife to a saw sharpener who lived on 30th Avenue near the theater. He shaped it into a double-sided dagger and sharpened both edges. I put it in a scabbard and wore it on my belt. The next time that dog attacked me I could defend myself. I didn't have too long to wait. I went to visit someone near the collie's motel. As I rounded the corner of the motel the collie was waiting. My nemesis stood snarling at me with fully bared teeth. I slowly pulled my knife out and held it straight in front of me. The dog inched closer. I yelled at it. It didn't move.

I yelled louder to the house, "Come get your dog."

The collie took another inch forward and rumbled in its throat. I was truly scared.

I yelled louder, "I'm going to kill your damn dog. I'm going to kill the son of a bitch. I'm going to kill it, kill it…" I continued, never taking my eyes off the hated dog.

The dog's child hating mistress came out and yelled at me.

"What's going on?" She demanded.

"Call your damn dog."

She saw the knife in my hand and called the dog.

Then she said, "I'm calling the sheriff."

"Go Ahead. Call the cops. I dare you. I hope they take your damn dog away."

She and the dog went in the house. I was shaken and went home. I told Mom and asked her to call the sheriff. But she didn't think we should. The good thing was, I never saw the dog again.

When Grandpa Was a Kid

Chapter 23

Betty's Cafe

In the winter when the school bus reached my stop, it was already dark. I often walked home alone in the rain. If no one was home I would find things to occupy myself until Mom or Virgil came home from work. Sometimes when I had a little money, I'd get my pack of damp cigarettes from behind the house and head for Betty's Café.

Betty's Café was close by and a good warm place to go. It was a low roofed, two-story house that faced Highway 99. The café was downstairs and an apartment was upstairs where Dick Miller's Mom now lived alone. There was usually a truck or two parked in the ample gravel lot out front. Sometimes they lined the roadside.

Betty served homemade pie and strong coffee, dished up with a trucker's vocabulary to match that of her clientele. She had more crust than her pies, but on the inside she was a cream puff. She always had a soft smile for me. Occasionally, Mom waited tables for her. Mavis tried working for her but couldn't take the foul language. I, on the other hand, liked being around grown men. I tried to emulate them. Sometimes when Mom was working at the cafe, she would seat me at a table for a piece of pie or maybe even dinner. But when she wasn't there, I sat at the counter and postured like the truck drivers I admired.

Men would walk in late in the afternoon and say,

"Gimmie a cup a coffee an' a roll a nickels". They would set the coffee on the glass top of the horse race pinball machine and break open the nickels. Most who played would put in several nickels to increase their odds and better the jackpot, and then start shooting balls. They hammered and bumped the machine with the heels of their hands trying to coax the balls into the right holes. Some guys talked to it, "Come on, come on, easy does it." The trick was not to tilt it. If it tilted everything was lost, then the talk wasn't so gentle. The object was to move lights across the glass display above the front of the machine by sinking balls in holes with matching lighted numbers.

There were levels to reach that paid off in nickels. Show and Place were winners, but Win was the jackpot and could yield a lot of nickel. Nickels were spit into a fist-sized square hole at the bottom of the machine, *cachunk, cachunk* ... , two nickels at a time. When a jackpot was hit, the cachunking kept going and going. The hole filled up and started spilling out on the floor. Two nickels at a time could take a while. By the time it was done, everyone in the café was watching the proud gambler gather his nickels. Usually at the end of the payout, a hatful of nickels was set on the counter. The waitress counted them, and gave folding money to the winner.

I was too young to play pinball, but when I got older that's what I wanted to do. In the meantime I was learning how men behaved at the café,

One evening after school I walked in from a cold rain and sat at the counter. The warm air smelled good

Betty's Cafe

to a hungry kid. The TV behind the counter was turned down low.

"How are ya Paul?" asked the waitress.

"Gimmie a cup a coffee – black!" I sat up a little straighter and looked serious. I was 14-years old. "What kind'a pie ya got?"

"Apple, loganberry, cherry, banana cream and Boston cream."

It was always the same.

"Banana cream."

I sipped my coffee, letting the cup warm my hands, watched TV and picked slowly at my pie. Pretty soon I lit a cigarette and listened to the action at the pinball machine. I wasn't much of a smoker, but that's what men did. I smoked it down and, like a real man, butted it out in my coffee cup.

The waitress returned and asked, "More coffee?"

"Fill'er-up!"

I sipped my coffee until I sucked in my cigarette butt. It and a mouth full of coffee spewed back into the cup. Surprised and humiliated, I glanced quickly around to see if anyone noticed. My face was getting warm. I hurriedly slapped enough change on the counter, and slipped quietly back into the rain.

When Grandpa Was a Kid

Chapter 24

Old Music and a New Baby

In the early days of traveling by car, motels popped up along the newly paved highways. These motels were usually built as tiny one-bedroom cabins with a combination kitchen and living area with a separate bedroom and bath. Some were connected in a row by little door-less, dirt floored garages in between. After World War II, newer motels made the tiny originals obsolete.

Many of the old motels became cheap housing that rented by the week or month. It was to just such a cabin, on the West Valley Highway in Kent, that Mavis brought her new baby in February 1953.

I waited out front, shooting darts at a board with my air pistol while Mom and Virgil were inside helping Mavis and her new baby get settled in. My only experience with newborns was with cats, so when Mom came out I asked, "Are its eyes open?"

Mom laughed at me and said, "Come on in and see for yourself."

I was surprised that the baby's eyes were open. Otherwise, the baby looked like any other baby, but this one was my new nephew Clifford. He looked great.

After a while, the new Adams family moved again to a similar motel apartment on the East Valley Highway just south of Kent. Mavis was home alone with the baby while Ernie was busy sitting out a six-month sentence in the King County jail, the same jail where my bus driver Deputy Simms worked nights. Ernie was thrown in the slammer when he got caught stealing a pistol from Schoff's Sporting Goods store in Kent. He waded in during a flood and was arrested for looting.

One Saturday evening I went with Mom and Virgil to visit Mavis. When we got there, a couple of young men were there and one was drinking beer. Mavis perked a fresh pot of hot coffee for everyone. As soon as it was served little Clifford reached up and grabbed a cup, spilling it into his shoe. He screamed and everyone jumped to his aid. I just stood and stared, watching the young man with the beer immediately pour it into Clifford's shoe. Thanks to some quick thinking Clifford was not burned.

During Ernie's absence, I made a few rather long bicycle trips to see Mavis. On one of my trips through Kent, I went to a secondhand store that had hundreds of old 78 speed records. I took several home tied to the rack on my bike. These made great targets for my BB gun. Bob tossed one in the air and I shot at it. It broke apart when the BB struck it. They shattered when thrown against trees, and flew apart when they hit the pavement on 30th Avenue in front of our house.

After destroying most of them, I played the few that remained. It was fun to hear the strange old songs. One song was from World War I, recorded in 1918 called, "Good Morning Mr. Zip-Zip-Zip." I loved to hear the fast paced chorus of this ancient song, "...Ashes to ashes, and dust to dust, if the Camels

Old Music and a New Baby

don't get you the Fatimas must..." I could imagine a bunch of soldiers with short haircuts smoking Camels and Fatimas while sitting in the cold mud of bombed out trenches. I knew about this war because I had watched "All Quiet on the Western Front" at the Richland Theater.

A deep voiced cowboy with a Texas accent sang another song. It was a beautiful old negro hymn called, "Steal Away". His slow smooth baritone voice sang, "Steal away, steal away, steal away to Jesus!" It had a gentle sadness to it that I had not heard in music. I sat on the front porch and played this song over and over.

When Ernie got out of jail he and Mavis moved to yet another old motel. This one was less than a block from the Midway Drive-In. Since we were almost neighbors, I became a frequent visitor.

A couple of doors down lived a young couple with a new baby. She was a songwriter, and Patty Paige had made one of her songs popular the year before. The young woman's husband piloted for the Flying Tiger Line. During the war, he flew P-40 fighters for China in the American Volunteer Group nicknamed the Flying Tigers. Those were the planes with the white-toothed sardonic smiles painted on the engine cowling.

I asked Mavis, "What are these people doing living in an old motel cabin?"

She didn't know, but thought the cause was alcoholism. One night I reluctantly volunteered to watch their baby so they could go somewhere. They came home hours after they said they would reeking of booze. Mavis was right.

Chapter 25

Bow Lake Farm

When Dad got out of the hospital after his logging accident, he went into partnership with Victor Colacurcio running greenhouses on the Bow Lake Farm across from the Seattle Tacoma International Airport. Vic's brother Frank owned the farm, and their parents and little brother Pat, lived there. Dad was a friend of Vic's dad. It was a simple partnership. The Colacurcio's provided the greenhouses and Dad provided the management and labor. They split the profits.

Summer finally came. The Federal Way School District saw fit to promote me to the eighth grade. With time on my hands, I decided to visit my dad. I walked the whole five miles to the farm and spent the day following my dad around as he did his work. That day he made a knife. He had some used industrial hacksaw blades about fourteen inches long that might have been an inch-and-a-half wide. We took them to a rugged little workshop where Dad used a grinder to shape the knife. When the blade was ready he cut a two-piece wooden handle, drilled two holes in the blade and bolted everything together. He finished it by oiling the handle and sharpening the blade. This metal held a good sharp edge.

Then he asked, "Do you want to make one?"

"Sure," I said.

He carefully instructed me. While I worked, Dad

showed me a small bald spot on the crown of his head.

"Do you know how I got that?" he asked.

I stared at the spot. "Looks like you're losing your hair," I said.

"Oh no! I leaned too close to the drill press and it yanked a chunk out, and I can tell you it hurt like hell."

This was one of his not so true stories, but it served the purpose of warning me not to get my mop of hair too close to the machines. He didn't need to tell me. I vividly remembered Mom telling me that her employer at the Diamond Caulk and Horseshoe Company in Duluth hung a woman's scalp over the front door for just such a reminder.

On the way home that afternoon I hacked at grass and limbs with my new knife. At home, I asked if I could spend some time with my Dad. Mom agreed. I packed up all my comics, some personal stuff, my BB gun and my bicycle.

A long narrow driveway sloped down from 188th Street between fallow fields to a large farmyard. The Colacucio's lived in a twenties era three-story brick house across a wide gravel yard from a low barn. Near the house, were two greenhouses joined side by side. Each house was 120 feet long and 60 feet wide, with a 10-foot wide seed-starting house joined to it on the side next to the yard. Across the yard from the greenhouses was a two-story, six-stall, equipment garage. Dad lived upstairs.

Dad and I walked up the stairs to a narrow hallway that ran to a window on the far end. There were five doors on each side of the hall, each opened into a small room ten feet by ten feet. These had once been rooms for farm workers. The first two rooms had the wall between them cut out to make a combination kitchen and bedroom for my dad. The kitchen had a sink, a hot plate, a beautiful antique round oak table and some matching chairs. Across the hall, a corner room was converted into a bathroom. Its two large windows were covered by sheets

"Go find yourself a room," Dad said.

"Which one?" I asked.

"Any one you like."

I looked at the remaining rooms. I chose the corner room overlooking the yard. It had a view of the farm, part of Bow Lake, and SeaTac Airport. I dragged in a single bed from another room and made it up with sheets and blankets from home. I found three wooden orange crates and set them on end and stacked my comics in them. My clothes were hung on some nails that were driven into the wall, and my BB gun stood against the wall next to my bed. I was moved in.

Dad fixed dinner on his hot plate. Most of his meals were meat, bread and potatoes. That's probably what we had that night.

I once asked him, "Why don't you eat more vegetables and salad?"

He told me, "You'd have to eat a bushel of that stuff, to get any good out of it."

He found mushrooms growing under the benches in the green houses and fried them for dinner. I was scared of them and wouldn't submit to even a taste. I remembered conversations back home in Grandma

Strand's kitchen about toadstools and mushrooms and how dangerous they were.

The next morning I awoke to the smell of bacon. After a quick breakfast, we went to work in the greenhouses. Dad showed me how to water, so I spent a considerable amount of time dragging hoses around and pouring water onto the benches. The benches were made of two-by-twelve redwood planks, four planks on the bottom and one on each side and end. The benches were filled with manured earth. They were close together and filled the houses. Water dripped from between the planks and onto the dirt floor.

Cucumber vines were tied up on wires that stretched the length of each bench and to a wire grid about seven feet above the dirt floor. The plants hung from the wire grid forming a canopy overhead, with cucumbers hanging down waiting to be picked.

To pick the cucumbers, a wooden box was placed so that each end was sitting on a bench, and the box straddled the aisle. All the harvester had to do was push the box forward and fill it with produce. Because of all the plants, the greenhouse air had extra oxygen. Working in that rich air gave me a good feeling.

The greenhouse itself was made out of squares of glass. The whole thing was glass, down to the foundation, which stood the height of the benches. At the peak of the roof were glass ventilation doors the length of the greenhouse that could be opened to let hot air escape, or a breeze blow in. Chains manipulated them. Dad adjusted these occasionally during the day. High above the benches were rows of lights. On one end of each house was a little door that opened to a beehive. The bees were for pollinating. Each house had a thermostat that controlled the hot water furnace.

Next to the greenhouses stood a small building with two ten-foot square rooms for supplies. It had a basement with an oil-burning boiler that supplied hot water to the greenhouses.

There were two broken glass panels in the greenhouse. I guess the temptation for some kid to throw a rock at all that glass was overwhelming.

"I don't know why the glass gets broken, but I have to replace it," Dad said.

He got two new pieces of glass from one of the boiler house storerooms and propped a ladder against the greenhouse. With a special greenhouse ladder on his shoulder, he climbed up to a gutter between the seed-starting house and the roof of the greenhouse, and then carefully walked out to the middle, with glass both beside and below him.

"Be careful," I yelled. But he ignored me.

He placed the special ladder on the glass canopy of the main greenhouse. He carefully worked his way up to a broken panel and replaced it. I was waiting for him to pass out and fall through the glass to the benches below. He replaced both panels without incident.

It was late June and the greenhouses were getting hot. Dad gathered some buckets and other things together.

"What are you doing now?" I asked.

"We need to throw on some whitewash to keep the heat out," Dad said.

"I thought you needed sunlight to grow plants," I said.

"Don't need quite so much. It's getting too hot to work."

He mixed a bag of whitewash with some water in a small barrel. Then he put a ladder up to the same gutter he walked on to fix the glass, and climbed up carrying a pail of whitewash and an empty soup can. This looked even more risky than the glass repair. There he stood, stiff backed on a narrow rain gutter with a pail in one hand, and a can in the other. I got a little frightened. *Should I stay here and watch, or go inside in case he falls through and needs my help?*

"Hey! What are you waiting for?" he yelled. Grab a pail of whitewash and give a hand."

"What? You want ME up THERE?"

"We don't have all day. Get up here and, make it snappy."

I obeyed. I stood on the gutter at the top of the ladder, bent over with my fingers pinching the narrow rail between the columns of glass. Below me I could see, pipes, lights, a network of support wires and a green blanket of cucumber vines. I began to shake. Dad had walked all the way down to the other end.

"Straighten up!" he yelled, "What's the matter with you?"

"This is kind of scary," I yelled back, "I don't think I can do it."

Bow Lake Farm

Dad was hard of hearing and I realized that he hadn't heard a word I said.

Dad yelled some instructions. "Do what I do and I'll meet you in the middle."

He dipped his can in the pail and started throwing whitewash all over the glass, covering it evenly.

On wobbly feet, I dipped my can in the pail and slowly straightened up. I threw the whitewash hard up the side of the glass. It went almost nowhere. Fear gripped me and I thought I was going to fall. I quickly squatted down and stared at what fate was waiting below. I would crash through the glass and land on the wire web above the cucumbers. I would hang there bleeding to death from my many lacerations, as the wires cut waffle patterns into my skin. The song, "Steal Away" passed through my mind. This wouldn't be stealing away. This would be a wretched and painful death lying spread-eagle on the cucumbers.

"Hey! Are you going to sit there all day, or get some work done?"

My fear turned to anger. I again dipped my can in the pail and threw it at the glass. I did it again. I was whitewashing the glass. But before I got a good start, Dad met me and that side of the greenhouse was done.

Dad finished the rest as I watched.

Not everything was work. Most of the time, I could do whatever I wanted. I had a new Walt Disney comic, the big twenty-five-cent summer issue. On the cover was a picture of Donald Duck and his three nephews driving up a mountain road in a little round convertible headed for Yosemite National Park.

When Grandpa Was a Kid

Comics to a kid bring reality to imagination. I could feel myself being pulled into those mountains as I joined the adventure. Far away, at SeaTac, I could hear an airplane revving its engines for takeoff. I sat on my bed and studied the pictures while slowly reading the words until my adventure was over.

Twice a week, about midmorning, the Golden Rule Bakery truck pulled into the barn yard and sounded its horn. Dad could be counted on to buy cinnamon rolls or butterhorns. We sat right down and ate some, and then got back to whatever we were doing. There was plenty left for breakfast the next day.

Dad's partner, Victor Colacuccio, usually came around in the late afternoon after he got off work as a cement truck driver, to help around the greenhouses. Vic liked to pick a cucumber and peel it with his pocketknife while the three of us stood between the benches and talked. Vic's face always had a friendly smile, and he was a good conversationalist. He was one of the most industrious people I ever met Sometimes he had his older one-ton flat bed truck sitting out in the yard loaded with pea gravel, for a delivery he would make as soon as he left the farm. At other times he and my dad would do lawn installation or concrete patios. I went along on a couple of those jobs.

Nights on the farm were simple. Sometimes after dinner, Dad would go talk with Mr. Colacuccio and drink a little of his Italian wine. But usually, after a late dinner, dad would lie in his bed to rest his painful back. He read the paper or maybe a novel. We often talked about things until I went to bed. Sometimes I could hear him playing his violin just like he did years before.

Mr. Colacurcio did assembly work at the Kenworth Truck Company in Seattle. He came home at night in a nice, but older, International Harvester pickup truck. He liked to spend his evenings sitting at the kitchen table after dinner, sipping dark red Italian wine. I called him Mr. Colacurcio out of respect, but it seemed like everyone else called him "old man."

Mrs. Colacurcio spent a lot of time in her kitchen. She was a good cook and a good mother. On Sundays, she had her children and their families come home for dinner. Dad and I were often included. She served delicious Italian food. A gallon of homemade Italian wine sat on the table.

Old man Colacurcio made his own wine – barrels of it. Just down the hill from the house was a wine cellar, dug into the hillside. The earth helped control the temperature. Even in the summer, it was cool inside. Large barrels of wine sat on the sides of the cellar filled with the wine that the family drank. There were also cases of the same wine in bottles with wax sealed corks. I occasionally saw one of these bottles on my dad's table. There was more than wine in that cellar. Up against some barrels, was a short row of shiny one-armed bandit slot machines, the nickels and quarters still showing in their little front windows. I wanted to pull some change out of my pocket and start playing, but I knew better than to ask if I could touch one. I imagined having one in my room that I could play whenever I wanted. I also knew they were illegal and weren't something to talk about.

Frank Colacurccio, Vic's brother, owned the farm and the slot machines. Frank also owned a couple of hotels in Seattle and was rumored to provide illegal entertainment including gambling. Dad and I sometimes ate dinner at one of those hotels where Frank hung around the cash register with a cigar in his mouth. He always greeted us with a polite smile.

Down the hill from the wine cellar was a peat bog. In addition to greenhouse farming, Vic and my dad were dredging peat from the bog and selling it by the truck load. They called it humus. They also used it for the lawns they planted.

Dad and Vic had a company truck. It was a new 1953 Golden Jubilee edition Ford dump truck. They used it mostly to deliver humus. Sometime dad used it to deliver produce or get supplies. One Saturday morning I was taken along in it, to help Vic move his maternal grandparents into a small house, almost a cottage, near the wine cellar. The grandparents lived on a farm across the Duwamish River from the Boeing Airplane Company's main plant in Seattle. The farm had been sold to Boeing for a parking lot expansion. Everything on the farm was old and unpainted.

Vic's grandparents were a hardy Italian couple who came from Sicily many years before. At a hundred years of age, they were still married. We loaded several things in the truck and went back to the Bow Lake Farm.

The youngest Colacurcio, Patrick, had some

friends over one day, and I joined them as we looked around the farm for something to do. In the barn we found several large boxes of rubber bands that had once been used for farm produce. They were long and stretched about two feet. We ran around shooting each other with them – they hit hard. Then I noticed a pile of lathe stacked in the back of a long abandoned model T pickup that was partially buried in junk in the center of the barn. We nailed two strips of lathe onto a handle and had powerful double-barreled rubber band guns, two feet long. We blasted each other until one of the kids got hit in the eye.

Also abandoned in the barn were pinball machines, the horse race kind like at Betty's Cafe. They belonged to Pat's brother Bill, who operated a pinball business. My usual reticence to ask for things was overcome by my desire to play a pinball machine. To my delight, I got the necessary permission to actually take one. Pat and some other kid helped carry it up the stairs. It went into an empty room next to mine. It had electrical problems and could not be plugged in, but since most of the machine was mechanical I was able to fix it up into working condition. The shooting device was spring loaded and worked fine. The balls were set into play by pushing a lever. But there were no lights, and although I shot balls onto the playing table and bounced them against the pins so they fell into the holes, it lacked the ability to take nickels and spit out jackpots.

On more than one occasion, Pat and I bicycled to the SeaTac Airport. We found comic books left lying on chairs by travelers and took them. It was also fun to walk around the terminal and see airplanes up close. We decided to ride our bikes on the runway. All that concrete was irresistible. While we were riding around in circles in front of the terminal, a loudspeaker came on.

"You kids get off the runway."

We headed back toward the terminal. Again the loudspeaker blasted,

"Get those bikes off the runway!"

Then a car started coming our way. Afraid of trouble, we peddled fast for the end of the runway, across the grass and down a dirt trail to 188th Street. We got away.

The whole Calocuccio family showed up for the Forth-of-July. Mrs. Culacurccio and her daughters made a big dinner. The kitchen was full. Outside, fireworks were blasting.

A car was leaving to get more fireworks. Dad handed me some serious cash and told me to go along. Fireworks were illegal in King County, but just south of Federal Way, in Pierce County, you could buy all the fireworks you wanted. At the county line, we could see long rows of fireworks stands and scores of parked cars, on both sides of Highway 99. I stood at the high counter and made my order.

"Gimmi ten packs of Zebra fire crackers, a couple of boxes of two-inch fire crackers, a pack of bottle rockets, and some punks."

I also bought skyrockets, aerial bursts, buzz bombs, ground rockets, Roman candles and a big box

Bow Lake Farm

of assorted fireworks. I even had a little cash left over. Dad didn't like to look cheap in front of his Italian friends.

We spent the rest of the day setting off firecrackers, chasing each other with ground rockets and blowing-up anything we could. That evening the farm lit up with our many skyrockets, while the men sat around the yard drinking wine, and the women peeked out of the windows.

I found an old water faucet on the ground with a three-inch pipe attached. It looked like a gun so I put a firecracker down the pipe, and then stuck a stone in after it for a bullet. I held it by the faucet just like an old time muzzleloader. I aimed it at the garage. The fuse stuck out the front and I lit it. Boom! I felt a searing pain and dropped the faucet. The palm of my hand was scorched. I spit on it and jumped around until the pain subsided. I hadn't thought to shut off the faucet. With the faucet turned off, I repeated the action and shot a stone into the siding of the garage. I shot at other more suitable targets until I found something else to do.

Any time Dad needed something from the store, he sent me to get it. Just little things like butter or cigarettes. One morning he needed gas and cigarettes so he gave me a five-gallon can and told me to get some gas. It was just under a mile to the tiny Bow Lake Grocery. The store was across Highway 99 on the corner of 188th street. Two gas pumps stood in front. Since there wasn't much traffic on 188th, a pressure sensitive black rubber panel was placed flat on the road that, when depressed, would change the traffic light so cars could cross Highway 99. No cars were around, so I jumped on the rubber panel until the light changed, then I crossed the Highway.

I walked in the store and said, "Hi, my dad wants three gallons of regular and a pack of Luckys."

"Sure. You got a note for those cigarettes?" asked the storekeeper.

"Sure," I said, and handed over the note.

A five-gallon can with three gallons of gas weighs close to twenty pounds. That doesn't sound like much until you carry one uphill for awhile. The wire handle started cutting into my hand and my arms started to weaken. I switched hands several times until both were tired out, and then I sat on the gas can to rest. I repeated this several times before finally getting back to my dad.

"What took you so long?" he wanted to know.

I had a long stay at the farm, but eventually it was time to go. I was going to miss my bedroom with its view and Dad's cooking. I would long remember some of the things we did together, like driving home one night from Mavis' place through a valley blanketed with fog. I had to walk in front of the headlights signaling which way to turn so we wouldn't drive the truck into the Green River. I would miss the steaks we ate at Frank Colacurcio's hotel restaurant, after selling a truckload of cucumbers. And I would miss the greenhouses.

When I got home the first thing I saw was a brand new 17-inch Philco television set.

"Where's my TV?"

"We traded it in for a nice new one," Mom said.

Gone! My beautiful television was gone, and nobody even asked me. The realization sunk in. It never was mine.

When Grandpa Was a Kid

Chapter 26

Displaced by Fire and Jealousy

We received the news that Grandma and Grandpa Landgren's farm had burned to the ground. A spark from a chimney started the shingle roof burning, and a strong wind sped the flames across the farm buildings. The house, barn, horse barn, creamery, everything was gone. Grandma and Grandpa fought the fire alone, saving only a few of their belongings. Coincidentally, the farm burned just when Grandpa retired. Fortunately, it was well insured. After that, they decided to come west and join us in Midway. They arrived in Grandpa's 1948 Studebaker pickup with all their remaining belongings in the back.

I didn't have to wonder where they would live. Virgil was going back to work at Hanford. Our home was sold to my grandparents. Virgil bought a 1953 Kit trailer house and parked it in the driveway. It was five feet longer than our old one and much nicer, but it would be back to sleeping on the couch again.

School started without me. I would wait until we got back to the big trailer park in North Richland and enroll there. I spent my remaining days in Midway watching TV and hanging around Betty's café. A gambling law had been passed and the horse-race pinball machine was gone, replaced by a dime machine that didn't pay out. Only an electronic dinging sound announced a win. A little counter, like an odometer, kept track of the winnings. When the player finished, any winnings could be collected from the waitress. Boring. But the pie was still good. We finally left for Richland.

Our new trailer was parked on a corner lot on the other side of George Washington Way, about a half mile from where we lived before. Other than that, not much was different. I tried to find some kids I used to know, but they had moved away. My new school was the Chief Joseph Junior High School in Richland. Chief Joseph was a well respected Nez Perce Chief best known for his long resistance to the U.S. Government's attempts to restrict his people to a reservation. The cavalry chased his people all over Eastern Washington, Idaho and Eastern Oregon. When they finally caught him he said, "From where the sun now stands I will fight no more forever." He got a junior high school named after him.

The school was built three years earlier by General Electric and lacked nothing. It had a theater complete with a balcony and a projection room. Across the hall was a snack bar and down the hall were fully equipped wood and metal shops. The place was beautiful – for a school. It was built to take the load off Carmichael, the other junior high school in Richland.

Getting a late start in school meant I got whatever classes were still available, whether I liked them or not. Among others, I was given shop and drama. My first shop project taught me to select wood stock, use a band saw, sander and drill press. I had to select a piece of wood three feet long and turn it into a swat paddle. I cut, drilled and sanded until the paddle was done. I

Displaced by Fire and Jealousy

burned my name on it and stood it in a row of paddles next to the shop teacher's office door. The teacher called it his "board of education".

It wasn't long before I found out how these things were used. A boy in metal shop welded a handle onto something, and then left it unattended before it was cool. Another kid, who had no way of knowing the handle was hot, grabbed it and burned the palm of his hand. After delivering the injured student to the nurse, the shop teacher escorted the offending welding student to the stock room. Another teacher was brought in as a witness. Listening through the open stock room door, the rest of us heard everything.

"Get your paddle," the shop teacher ordered.

Then came the next order. "Bend over and put your hands on your knees."

After a short pause, "Ooow!" a deep male voice yelled.

We heard the paddle rattle around on the floor. Then through the open door:

"You think you're pretty smart, don't ya? Now you're gonna get two swats," the shop teacher yelled. "Now grab your knees and don't move."

Then, whack! The paddle struck home, then another "whack", and the welding student ran out the door yelling obscenities as he disappeared down the hall and out of the school. The next day someone asked him what had happened.

"I jumped to one side and the paddle hit the other teacher" he said.

Drama was easy, except I had stage fright. Our

first play had me cast as a palace guard with a big spear. My role was to stand at attention next to a paper pillar, as my anxiety built. Finally, all eyes were on me as I said my only line, "Here he comes now!" Total fear. I was referred to as an actor.

I fell back into the routine I had followed three years earlier. I went to movies alone at night and caught the army bus to Richland, and sometimes Pasco or Kennewick, to go shopping or just look around. Sometimes I hung around the drugstore and drank strawberry ice cream sodas. On weekends Mom and Virgil would take me with them for shopping and sightseeing. We even went to a movie together. We saw *The Glen Miller Story* at the Kennewick Theater.

On a sunny Saturday afternoon, I bicycled into Richland where a crowd gathered in the parking lot of the Uptown Richland Shopping Center. A car was being raffled off. I had two tickets. A lot of time went by while lesser items were raffled off and speeches were made. We finally got to the car. I wanted the car even if it was a Dodge business coupe. Somebody was on stage with his hand on a crank turning a big wire mesh basket. Hundreds of tickets tumbled in the sunshine. I began to pray and make deals with God for that car. The basket stopped turning and a little side door was opened. *Please let it be my ticket.* A hand reached in and slowly dug around for a ticket. The winning ticket was held out for everyone to see. The master of ceremonies read off the first number. I had it. He read off the second number. I had that too. Then I had the third. I was winning. I didn't have any of the

Displaced by Fire and Jealousy

rest of the numbers. Someone else was heading for the stage waving his end of the winning ticket. It turned out every one had the same first three numbers. It was the remaining numbers that were different. Oh well, what could a fourteen-year-old do with a car? *Anyway, when I'm old enough to drive, I'll have a '49 Ford,* I thought.

It was fall and the winds blew hard up the Columbia River, hard enough to propel a neighbor boy and me up the street in a wagon. All we had to do was sit in his wagon with our coats held open to the wind. One night, the wind got worse. In the morning the trailer next to ours had blown over and was sitting at a cockeyed angle against a post. The people who lived there were from Alabama. They told us how it happened in their strange southern accent. Then they and some neighbors righted the trailer.

After school one afternoon, the boy with the wagon pulled something out of his pocket.

"I've got a box of .22 longs," he announced, and showed me a box of cartridges.

"Watch this," he said.

He picked out a cartridge and threw it as far as he could down the street. It popped when it hit the pavement.

"You can get into some real trouble with those things," I warned, "I know."

He pulled a slingshot out of his coat and shot a cartridge at the top of a water tower.

This gave me an idea.

The next afternoon I showed up with a long

When Grandpa Was a Kid

rubber band from a model airplane and a pocketful of fence staples. I rotated the handlebars of my bike up like a slingshot and attached the rubber band. I put a fence staple over the rubber band, grabbed it by the tips, and pulled way back past the rear tire. Whoosh, it was gone. I shot another one at the water tower. It ricocheted off the side. I had a real weapon. I practiced for awhile, and then the next afternoon I saw a crow on a wire. I took careful aim and fired. The staple hummed past and the bird flew away. I kept trying different targets till I lost interest.

I also discovered that I could throw a tire iron at things and stick the sharp end into just about anything. I had the tire iron sticking out of telephone poles, and could pop it through the half-inch plywood door on Virgil's shed. One day I was practicing throwing it in the air and sticking it in the ground, when it landed across the low power wires behind our trailer. A shower of sparks bounced the tire iron away from the wires, knocking out the lights on our block. I grabbed the tire iron and disappeared.

A little reflective thought caused me to abandon the tire iron as well as the staple slingshot. These things could only lead to trouble. I also stayed away from the kid with the .22 cartridges.

Mom took a job waiting tables at a nice restaurant in Uptown Richland. She didn't need to, but she loved to work and enjoyed being in public. Sometimes Virgil ate at the restaurant after he got off work, and hung around watching Mom. Other times he would just drop in for coffee. Later he accused her of flirting with

Displaced by Fire and Jealousy

other men. His jealousy was getting control of him.

He was also jealous of me. He and Mom had loud arguments about this. He thought Mom paid too much attention to me. When I wasn't around, they got along better. Suddenly I was on my way back to my dad's place.

I was allowed to take my dog, Bobby, and some clothes, nothing more.

When Grandpa Was a Kid

Chapter 27

A Greenhouse Winter

Things were different at the farm. A Japanese family had moved into rooms above the garage and remodeled the space into an apartment. Dad moved into the two small storerooms over the greenhouse boiler room. A bed, dresser, a small radio and a chair were in one room, his hot plate and a tiny table and chairs were in the other, along with some green house supplies. On the hot plate was a teakettle with copper tubing sticking out of the top and curling down to a cup.

"What's that?" I asked.

"I made cognac from some of Colacurcio's wine," Dad said.

"Does it work?"

"I got a few drops," he said.

Each room opened to the outside. In bad weather a coat was required to go to the next room. The only windows were in the doors. A crop of poinsettias was in the greenhouses.

The first morning was bacon and eggs. Dad sliced his bacon from a slab and cooked it first. Then he cooked the eggs in a pool of hot bacon fat.

"I like the way you fry eggs," I said.

"Mom's eggs are crispy on the outside and runny on the inside. I don't eat them."

"The secret is low heat," he said.

A pecking knock sounded at the door, followed by

"Quack-quack".

"What's that?" I asked.

"Oh, that's Donald. He wants his breakfast."

Dad opened the door and a plump white duck with a yellow bill looked up at him.

"Quack."

Dad slid a fried egg onto the concrete step. Donald ate it. Bobby watched.

At night the dark filled with noises from the boiler below. The thing made rumbling noises and pipes made popping noises. It was easy to imagine it blowing up through the floor. Sometimes when it got too noisy, Dad got out of bed to go check the gauges.

I always asked, "Is it okay?"

"You bet. It was just getting a little too hot," he'd say.

I got him to admit that if it got too hot and started boiling it could explode.

Pat, who lived on the farm all his life, told me that several years earlier, a single man with a vivid imagination lived in one of these rooms. At night the boiler made strange noises that scared him. Then one night when he thought it would explode, he bolted from the room and ran into the woods beyond the peat bog, and never came back. Was Pat putting me on? The only thing that let me sleep at night was reasoning that if my dad wasn't worried about it, neither was I.

I went with Pat to the bus stop at the end of the driveway on 188th Street. It took us to Puget Sound Junior High, where to my delight, school was half days. Instead of lunch we went home to make room for the afternoon students. I barely remember this school. I know it was the first junior high school in the Highline district, but what I did there is long forgotten. What I do remember is getting on and off the school bus. We got on in the predawn light and got off in the early afternoon.

I spent most of my afternoons hanging around the greenhouses with my dad. Sometimes Vic came around and talked about different projects he had going. He was always enjoyable. I could sense he liked me.

One afternoon I went to the produce buyers with Dad. Farmers who did business with them were allowed to buy damaged cans of food by the lot. They were big cardboard boxes sold like grab bags. The cans were dented and many didn't have labels, but they were cheap so Dad bought two boxes. At home he put the boxes in the kitchen. After that it was a lottery what was to eat. Most of the cans were fruit and we ate a lot of plums, but sometimes what we thought were plums, might be figs or corn.

Another time I went there with Vic. It was late in the afternoon, and the warehouse workers were gone except for the buyers. Vic was talking about selling poinsettias. The warehouse was processing bananas, some of which were too ripe to send to the stores, but yellow and just right to eat. The buyer asked us if we wanted some.

Vic said, "sure."

The buyer said, "eat all you want, but we can't let you take any home."

When Grandpa Was a Kid

We stood around and pigged out on bananas, while Vic finished his business with the buyer.

As Christmas approached, Dad turned all the greenhouse lights on, day and night, to force the poinsettias to bloom. The farm glowed all night until the poinsettias were ready. Then it was time to sell. Each pot was wrapped with foil and put on the back of Vic's truck and taken to the produce buyer. When I got home from school the greenhouses were empty.

Christmas away from Mom made me homesick. It made me wonder why Dad never returned to Minnesota to see his mom or even write her a letter. But when Christmas came, he wired a poinsettia to his mother. My mom sent me a blue V-neck sweater. It was made of something synthetic, because it sparked so much that Dad turned out the lights when I took it off, so he could see the static electricity coarse through it. During the holidays Dad and I went to Seattle and ate steaks at one of Frank Colacurcio's hotels.

The Japanese family living above the garage invited Dad and me to join them for part of their traditional Japanese New Year feast. A long table was covered with all kinds of foods. None of which I recognized. There were colored rice dishes, black bean dishes, a variety of fish and rice balls. I can't remember the rest, but there was plenty. Some of the food tasted too strange to enjoy, some too sweet and some was delicious. We got a tour of the apartment. Some kid lived in my old room and there was no sign of the pinball machine.

It was time to switch crops to Easter lilies. But

A Greenhouse Winter

first, Dad decided to convert the boiler to steam. He wanted to use steam to sterilize the soil. He had a pile of pipe dumped next to the greenhouses.

One morning at breakfast I asked, "What are you going to do with all those pipes?"

"Steam will be piped into the greenhouses and run through the earth in the benches. The steam will come out of little holes in the pipes and make the soil hot enough to sterilize it."

I went to school and he began drilling holes.

The boiler had to be converted from a hot water boiler to a steam boiler. This didn't settle well with me. I thought steam was what Dad was trying to prevent, so the boiler wouldn't blow up. He drilled thousands of little holes in the pipes, and then fitted the pipes together. He buried them in the earth at the bottom of the benches to complete his ambitious task. Vic came and we all waited while Dad turned on the steam. After a while, a low moaning sound filled the green houses.

I looked at Vic and asked, "What's that sound?"

"That's the bugs dying," he said.

"There must be an awful lot of bugs," I said.

Days later it dawned on me that the sound was from stream rushing out of all those tiny holes, not from the screaming mouths of tiny bugs.

The boiler didn't behave well as a steam boiler. Our little room shook while popping and cracking sounds where heard beneath the floor. The steaming only lasted one night, and Dad spent most of that night in the boiler room. It was a long night. I thought the boiler would blow the building to pieces, and steam me alive like the bugs in the greenhouses. The next day, Dad converted the boiler back to hot water.

After Christmas break the school switched to afternoon classes, causing Pat and me to walk home in the pitch dark guided only by the farm's distant light. But one night when we got off the bus a heavy snow was falling. The ground was pure white and the lights from the greenhouses brightened the thick cottony snowflakes. I came out of the snow into a warm greenhouse where I saw Dad, along with a couple of ladies he'd hired busy planting Easter Lilly bulbs. He worked late that night.

The next morning the snow was deep. We kicked a path from the bedroom to the kitchen. Now full of puppies, Bobby waddled her short legs through our footsteps. Donald the duck ate her fried egg in the snow.

After breakfast we went to the greenhouses. Rows of hundreds of red clay pots filled the benches. It was heavenly warm. Later on I went back to the bedroom, and turned on the radio for school reports. *Oh please be closed.* Popular music played as I waited for word. Eddie Fisher was singing as I looked out the door window into the greenhouses watching Dad attend to his new crop. The song went, "Oh my Papa To Me he was so wonderful, …Gone are the days when he could take me on his knee…" I became nostalgic. Then the good news, "All Highline Schools closed." I burst out the door into the snow. I got Pat and we found a sled and started sliding down what hills we had. I found

A Greenhouse Winter

some boards and made a small sled based on a soapbox design. It had four runners and could be steered. Dad got in the spirit and went to the shop. "I'll make you a real sled," he said. He welded some pipes into a good sized, strong, steel sled. He sanded and polished the runners. It was fast, but it couldn't be steered. I took it down the hill from the farmyard to the bog. There was one slight turn halfway down. The sled refused to turn. I tried to turn it, but the snow was too deep. I kept trying, as the sled headed toward a five-foot high pile of bean poles, with their sharp ends aimed right at me, as I picked up speed. At the last second I rolled off of the sled as it buried itself in the poles. I slid to a stop next to the pile.

The snow stuck around for a few days. I discovered Bobby would ride the sled all by herself. All I had to do was set her in front of me on the sled, then slide off, letting her go it alone. Bobby went sailing down the slope, ears flapping in the wind. I ran along behind her and then we did it all over again.

One night, when the snow was gone,, I heard Bobby crying in her box. I got out of bed to find that she had given birth to a dead puppy. It was a very large puppy. There was a stench in the air, the same deathly smell I remembered from the dead horse I saw by the road years before. Bobby's round eyes looked up at me, as if I could do something to ease her pain.

"Bobby needs help," I said.

"Let's wait until morning," Dad said.

"No! She needs help now. What can we do?"

"Not much we can do now. We'll have to wait till the veterinarian is open."

"But she's in pain we have to do something."

I waited helplessly. Bobby whined and appealed to me for help. I stroked her head, but I could do nothing. No more puppies were born.

Morning came slowly. Dad found someone with a car, who took us to the vet. We pulled in the parking lot and Dad said, "Wait here. We'll go talk to the vet."

Dad and his friend disappeared into the clinic. Bobby lay still in her box. I waited and waited. Bobby stopped crying and settled down in her box. Finally Dad came out.

"It's too late," I whimpered, "Bobby's dead!"

I sat at the kitchen table and wrote Mom a letter.

Dear Mom,

Bobby died trying to have puppies that were too big. …I'm doing nothing in half day school….

I want to go home….

Love, Paul

In the greenhouses the lilies were sprouting and looking good. But, closed environments with only one variety of plant are easy prey for pests that can wipe out a whole crop overnight. Typically, Dad would have sprayed with Malathion or maybe Parathion. Both are strong insecticides that can harm humans, especially in a greenhouse. To avoid the lingering exposure to insecticides, Dad decided to fumigate with Cyanide gas. Cyanide will kill any kind of animal quickly, especially in the amount Dad planned to use.

A Greenhouse Winter

Then the green house could be aired out quickly, leaving it clear of any harmful insecticide residue. I had my doubts. He and Vic argued about using it. Vic wanted nothing to do with cyanide. "That stuff is too dangerous." he said.

"It's the best way to go." Dad said. "It's safer in the long run, and it will kill everything in there."

"I'm worried about you." Vic said. "How can you spread that around without breathing any of it?"

Dad produced a rubber mask with a circular filter on each side. "I've got a gas mask." He said.

"That's not a gas mask," I butted in, "that just filters stuff out of the air. Cyanide is a gas, it'll pass right through."

The fumigant works by evaporating from granules into gas as soon it touches air.

Regardless of our pleading, Dad was ready to go. The first thing he did was scare us half to death by prying open the cyanide can. Vic and I stepped way back. The can was full of little grey pellets the size of small buck shot. Dad set the lid back on the can, put on his useless mask and stepped through the greenhouse door. He walked to the far side of the next greenhouse where he took the lid off of the can, exposing the cyanide to the air. Then he began pouring it on the floor as he went quickly down every other isle. As he got close, we could see the gas rise from the floor where he had been.

"Run Dad, run!" I yelled.

"Cliff, hurry!" yelled Vic.

He was moving faster as he approached the door.

The greenhouses were filling with the poison gas. He dropped the empty can on the floor and burst through the door. He quickly pulled the door shut behind him and snapped a padlock. He came toward us tearing off his mask and breathing deep and fast as he staggered forward. He leaned against the boiler house wall and gasped for air.

"The gas mask didn't work. I could smell the gas coming through. I held my breath as long as I could," he explained, as he fought to catch his breath.

I thought any amount of cyanide would kill you on the spot. But maybe the odor precedes the lethal amount, or maybe he smelled something else.

Cyanide poisoning is similar to suffocation. This is because cyanide stops the cells of the body from being able to use oxygen which stays in the blood unabsorbed by the cells of the body. Since this condition is universal to all animals, every bug, spider and toad in the greenhouses suffocated and died.

Dad had breathed an insignificant amount of the poison, if any, and soon recovered. He was mostly just out of breath. However, had he tripped and fallen, no one could have saved him.

The greenhouses were not airtight. All that night I lay listening to the boiler rumble and sniffed at the air for any indication that cyanide would overcome us in our sleep. The next day, while I was at school, Dad held his breath and went to the greenhouses and cranked open the ventilation panels at the top of each house. No one noticed as the deadly gas escaped into the outside air of the farmyard. After a while, Dad was

A Greenhouse Winter

back working in the greenhouses.

By April, thousands of Easter lily blossoms filled the oxygen charged air with the most wonderful aroma I can possibly remember. In this pleasing atmosphere, the lilies matured, were wrapped in foil, and sent to market. Here's where Vic showed his genius for business.

Vic sat at the kitchen table complaining about the lousy price they got for the lilies.

"I couldn't get a better price," he said, "I tried."

"Our lilies are better than anybody else's," Dad said. "They're wider, greener and have more blossoms. It's what everybody wants."

"Well, the market's flooded." Vic said. Then he got a bright idea. "Let's buy them back and sell them ourselves."

"Oh, really?" Dad said, skeptically.

"Sure," Vic said. He was getting exited. "The price has gone down so much, that we can buy them back for less than what we sold them for. Then we can sell them ourselves."

Dad and Vic chewed on this idea for awhile. Finally, it was agreed that Vic would buy back the lilies.

Vic drove up with some of the lilies on the back of his flatbed truck.

"Hey Paul, you want to help me sell these?"

"Okay," I said and jumped in the truck. Where are the rest of the lilies?" I asked.

"They're still at the buyer's warehouse."

Our first stop was a tavern. Vic scooped up three

or four pots of lilies and went in.

Soon he stuck his head out of the door and yelled, "Hey Paul, bring me all you can carry."

I met Vic at the tavern door. Warm tavern air flowed out. I handed over the lilies and went back to the truck. In a few minutes, Vic jumped into the cab with a big smile on his face. We stopped at a few more taverns, and then returned to the farm.

Vic threw a stack of money on the kitchen table in front of Dad.

"Look at this, Cliff, I sold all of them. I'm going back for more tomorrow."

"Where did you sell them?" Dad asked.

"Taverns," Vic said. "All I had to do was tell these guys to take an Easter lily home to the wife, and they snapped them up. I sold them for more than the florists get."

The next day Vic went selling again, and after a couple of days he was back at the greenhouse wearing a bigger smile than ever. "Sold all the lilies," he announced.

"Already? Dad asked.

"The buyer had more orders than he could fill and couldn't find any more lilies. He offered me top money for our lilies."

"Did you take it?" Dad asked.

"No, I talked him into a better price, and then I took it."

The topic changed to tomatoes. Tomatoes grown in Seattle area greenhouses were packaged and shipped to Alaska where the price was always high. In

A Greenhouse Winter

just a few years jet airplanes would end the green house vegetable industry. Jets would get fresh vegetables from California and Mexico to Alaska faster and more economically than the current use of boats and prop driven airplanes.

When Grandpa Was a Kid

Chapter 28

Failure

After Easter, my request to go home was answered. I was back in North Richland, but life was different. While I was gone, Mom moved out on Virgil. We now lived in a tiny old trailer several blocks away. Mom said the little trailer was temporary. "We'll move back to Midway in a couple of months." Then she tried to explain. "Virgil is a good man and a good provider, but I just can't stand his jealousy and bitching. Gripe, gripe, gripe, all the time, I just can't live that way."

I remembered the heavy arguments that had turned happy days into gloom.

Other troubles beset Mom. Earlier in the year she applied for a job with the Atomic Energy Commission. After a background check she was denied the job, because they said she wasn't a citizen. The naturalization people threatened to deport her to Sweden. They told her she was an illegal alien. I began to worry. What would happen if Mom was sent to Sweden? Would I ever see her again? Would I go to Sweden too?

Mom was allowed to stay but had to enroll in naturalization classes and would eventually earn her citizenship. Many years later when Grandpa Landgren died, Mom's adoption certificate was found in the bottom of his old Swedish steamer trunk. It stated she was a citizen of the United States. Why didn't he give

When Grandpa Was a Kid

her that when she needed it?

I reenrolled in Chief Joseph Junior High and tried to fit back in, but I had no idea what was going on and couldn't focus on school. I had few friends so I spent a lot of my time doing things by myself. I went to a lot of movies, went bike riding and hung around home, or sometimes the drugstore.

Paul age 14 in North Richland

When the school year ended I was told I had flunked again. No one told me why, but if I had finished at Puget Sound Junior High I would have passed. School got out early. I angrily stole a bottle of India ink on my way out of the building. I stood in a crowd of kids waiting for our buses to pull up. I looked around to see who was watching. When I felt safe, I threw the ink bottle high into the air, smashing it against the tall concrete wall of the school theater. I instantly regretted it. But inside I kept telling myself, *they deserve it*.

Suddenly a teacher started yelling, "Who did that, who threw that?"

Kids started looking up at the big black blotch running down the clean concrete. Nobody looked

Failure

toward me. More teachers came out. The school buses arrived but no one was allowed to get on. The teachers went through the crowd and asked questions, still no one looked at me and no one asked me any questions. Finally the teachers were licked, and we got on the buses. *Serves them right*, I thought.

When my bus got to North Richland, I slid out of my seat and kicked open the emergency door in back. An alarm sounded and the bus came to an immediate stop. I could get in trouble for this, but I did it maliciously and couldn't care less what anybody thought. My education was ruined and to hell with school. I jumped to the pavement and ran toward the drugstore for lunch. Other kids poured out of the back of the bus, as I sprinted through the sagebrush, leaving trouble behind.

After finishing my Coke and French fries, I sat in the shade of a Dutch Elm tree in the park in front of the drug store, and read a comic book. It was a warm beautiful day and I was free.

On a sunny June Saturday, I went to see Virgil. He still lived in the sleek little Kit trailer. I took along a chocolate cake I had baked in Mom's tiny oven. Virgil had the habit of sitting forward in his chair with an elbow on his knee, and a Lucky Strike cigarette smoldering between his fingers. We ate cake and talked for awhile. In those days, I didn't know how to express my feelings to someone I cared for, so I just said, "I'll be see'n ya, Virgil," and left. I never saw him again.

When Grandpa Was a Kid

Chapter 29

Rats and Giant Ants

Mom decided to send me back to my dad. She didn't want to leave me alone while she was at work. "When I sell the trailer, I'll find a job in Midway," she said.

She arranged a ride for me with a friend who was going to Seattle. He was someone mom met through her work. My jaw dropped when he pulled up in a new 1954 Mercury Sun Valley hard top convertible. It had a green tinted Plexiglas sunroof that covered the whole front of the roof. The Plexiglas was surrounded with dark green metallic paint, above a light golden metallic body. As I got into car, the sun shined green on the rolled and pleated vinyl seats. I was traveling in style. Mom flashed me her beautiful loving smile and assured me, "Have a good time. I'll see you in a few weeks." She stood with her hand waving high in the air, until we were out of sight.

The driver was one of the young men that were busy building the nuclear processing facilities in the Hanford nuclear reservation. He was friendly and we talked about all kinds of things. When we stopped for lunch, I got out and stared at the chrome and metallic paint shining in the sunlight.

Just North of Kent, a narrow gravel road led from the West Valley Highway. It passed between pastures of horses and cattle to a smaller "S" curved road. Two dogs ran out from a small farmhouse to bark at us. The road ended in a large farm yard. I got out of the car.

Tall trees surrounded a little rental house, a large yard and a weathered old barn. The farm belonged to a widow who lived in a substantial house on the other side of the barnyard.

Dad and Mavis greeted me. Mavis' piano stood against the wall and Dad's round oak table was in the kitchen. It was soon dinnertime. Mavis knew how to cook. The joy of sitting around the table with my family lasted into the evening as we talked. Dad was having health problems and had to let the greenhouses go. He now lived with Mavis and Ernie and their two babies. Ernie was out of work again, and Mavis was pregnant with her third child. After dinner I curled up on the couch and went to sleep.

The next morning Mavis fixed pancakes and homemade syrup. Later in the day, I left with Ernie to go swimming at Steel Lake. After that, we drove around for a while and then returned home. Ernie *could* have been looking for work.

The old barn stood across the yard from the house. It had an open door in front and one like it on the other side. I looked through to the pasture beyond. A rat the size of a cat silhouetted itself in the doorway. Another one ran by. I ran in the house and told Dad.

"Want to have some fun?" he asked.

Then he got his .22-caliber rifle and told me to go shoot some rats. I lay down in the yard and aimed the rifle at the open barn door. As soon as a rat appeared, I shot it. After two shots the rats didn't show themselves anymore.

Rats and Giant Ants

That afternoon, I walked to Kent to see a movie. A science fiction thriller was playing called, "Them." I took a shortcut along the fence line that led straight to the West Valley Highway. After walking a ways, I hitched a ride and was soon in Kent. The movie was about a swarm of giant mutated ants that came out of the Nevada desert and started killing people. Before anyone saw them, a high pulsating noise and a crunching sound could be heard, then a giant ant, bigger than a moose, slowly attacked. This theme persisted as the ants spread death all the way to Los Angeles.

After the movie, I walked out into the twilight. I started home along Meeker Street until the sidewalk ended, and then continued on the edge of the road. By the time I reached the West Valley Highway the sun was gone, so were the moon and stars. I walked along the gravel shoulder where the only lights were from far away farm yards. The air was damp and cool. A slight breeze carried the scent of fresh cut hay. An occasional car sped by lighting my way, then darkness again. Then I froze in fear. Somewhere in the darkness a crunching sound was drawing near. In my mind I saw giant mutant ants, then a loud "Mooo!" I bristled under a surge of adrenaline. *Oh God I'm scared*, I prayed. A cow stood on the other side of a fence, almost invisible in the starless night. I continued on, shaking with anticipation as my imagination got out of control. I heard things moving, but could see nothing. I was so utterly alone in the dark, with frightful sounds everywhere.

When Grandpa Was a Kid

I turned and looked back toward Kent and the protection of light, which was now out of sight. I kept telling myself, *there's nothing out there but your imagination*. But things were moving in the dark. I could sense them. I wished I hadn't gone to the movie. Finally, the window lights of our farm house came into view. I ducked under the barbed wire fence and started up the fence line toward home. Then I heard the thunder of horses coming my way. I couldn't see them but they were coming fast. I spun and dashed back to the fence and dove between the strands of wire. I jerked to a stop, caught on a barb. I could hear the horses breathing and stomping as they approached. With a rip, I kicked loose and fell through the fence into the damp grass and mud. I jumped up and ran. I didn't stop until the horse pasture was well behind me, and my panic eased.

Now I had no option but to walk an extra half mile to our driveway. It was a long driveway that passed a neighboring farm where two big dogs patrolled their home. My fear of wolves and dogs had me petrified. Also, being mauled by a collie was fresh in my mind. The dogs saw me. They ran at me barking furiously. I froze. They stopped at my feet sniffing and barking at me, but they didn't touch me. I started moving slowly toward home. My heart was thumping so loud that I feared it would excite the dogs. They stayed close until I passed their yard. Then they stopped in the road and I carefully continued home.

When I walked into the house Dad took one look at my muddy, ripped clothes and said, "What happened to you?"

I tried to calm down, but couldn't so I blurted out, "The horses chased me and the dogs up the road attacked me."

Dad jumped off the couch and went for his rifle. "I'll kill those damn dogs," he said.

"No, no!" Mavis shouted.

"Don't do it," I said, "you'll go to jail."

"I don't give a damn, I'm shooting those dogs."

Eventually, Dad relented. By then I was more composed and told the whole story. I don't think they believed me. I could hear those damn ants for days.

When Grandpa Was a Kid

Chapter 30

Starting Over

Mom finally made her break from Richland. She found a waitress job at the Blockhouse restaurant in Midway near the intersection of Highway 99 and the Kent-Des Moines Road. Ernie drove me to the old motel cabins where he and Mavis had lived the year before. Mom now had a unit there. A few of my belongings were waiting for me in our tiny new home. Our life had reached a new bottom. *Why do we have to live in this dump?* I wondered. But it was summertime and I set off to make the best of it.

The old friends I had in Midway were either gone or not interested in me. So I just hung around places and made whatever friends I could find. The drive-in theater still let kids watch movies, and Betty's Café was still a good place to drink coffee. I eventually ran across a friend from the school I went to the year before. He told me about a job opening.

A half block away from our motel cabin was the Cornelius Dinner House. It was an old log house converted to a restaurant and painted white. It had a large gravel parking lot in front. I talked to the manager who hired me on the spot. He was picky about appearance. Slacks, white shirt and a neat clean haircut were required. I went out to the washhouse and filled a tub with hot water and scrubbed clean a pair of slacks and a white shirt. I hung them to dry and got a haircut

When Grandpa Was a Kid

I looked as proscribed when I showed up for work. The owner's name was Cornelius, but he asked me to call him Boss. He showed me around the restaurant and explained how things were done. He was only open three nights a week, and only served dinner. There were three menu items; Glazed ham, beef steak and Cornelius fried chicken. He made three kinds of tarts for desert; lemon, chocolate and cherry. He had a staff of three; a chef (him), a waitress and a kitchen helper (me). We started at three and worked until nine.

The boss led me to his chicken fryer. It looked like a grill with a lid. It fried chicken on both sides at the same time. He said, "I invented this fryer. It's manufactured and sold under my name."

I took a closer look. It had a little plate attached that said, "Cornelius Chicken Fryer."

"That's great Boss," I said.

While Boss started preparing the meat and vegetables, he set me to making tarts. It didn't take long to catch on. What took the most time was learning how to talk to the boss. "It's not 'Hey Boss' it's just Boss," he said. "Do you think you can remember that?"

"Yeah Boss," I said.

"It's not 'Yeah Boss' it's 'Yes Boss.' Watch your grammar."

"Yes Boss."

It was a busy night. Cornelius had a full house. I cleared tables, washed dishes and ran all over getting things for Boss. The waitress knew some of the patrons by name and was extremely polite. After the doors were locked, Boss asked me what I wanted to eat.

"Can I have the ham?" I asked.

"That's, 'May I have the glazed ham?'" he corrected.

He served me himself. It was delicious. I thanked him politely.

The next night was a rerun except I ordered chicken.

"May I have the Cornelius fried chicken, please?" I asked.

"Of course you may," he answered with a smile, and set about serving me.

"No wonder you have so many return customers, Boss. This chicken is good."

"Thank you. What kind of tart would you like?"

"I think lemon would go well with chicken," I said.

"Good choice," he beamed.

The next night was not a rerun. I decided three days were enough. After a few more grammar lessons and a wonderful meal of Cornelius fried chicken, I resigned.

The boy who told me about the Cornelius job was Louis Kerrey who lived a quarter mile off of the Kent-Des Moines Road, about a mile west of highway 99. At fifteen, he was the oldest of four boys. The youngest was only two and had a serious case of rickets. He walked with bowed legs as if his low-slung diaper was carrying a football. The house was a one bedroom shack that sat down from the road next to a canyon. A wood fired cookstove heated the place, and sanitation was the, now illegal, outhouse. A black mongrel spaniel hung around the unattended yard.

Louie moved out of their filthy little house a few years earlier into a tiny hut he built for himself. The little door was on level ground but the rest of it projected out over the canyon on two-by-four stilts. It had no windows bigger than a knot hole. He constructed it of scrap lumber that his dad brought home to feed the stove. Louie used the longest of these scraps, but none were quite long enough. He could stand up in it when he built it, but now he had to crawl through the door and walk on his knees. Cramped for space, he added another tiny room to one side on some more stilts. He invited me in. The place was clean and neat, but shook a little. It bothered me that the canyon dropped away below us. I ask Louis why he put it there. He said he liked the canyon.

Many of the canyons around Puget Sound are cut from soft soil by water that's been running down them since the end of the ice age. They all had the same things in common, soft soil, big trees and a creek at the bottom. Larger canyons often had tributary canyons. Because of the steep topography, loggers usually left them alone. Consequently, large fir, maple, alder, a variety of other trees, and dense foliage gave these canyons a primal beauty.

It was over such a canyon that Louie's little hut hung.

Louie's dad worked nights in Seattle, leaving

Starting Over

Louie's mom alone with him and the other unruly siblings. Louie invited me over to spend the night. As soon as his mom turned out the lights we snuck out of the little hut to his dad's spare car. Louie had a key. Sometimes the car didn't start, so it was parked by the road ready to coast down the hill for a clutch start. We got in the old 1942 ford sedan and quietly coasted away.

Once out of earshot of the house, Louie let out the clutch and the car started. We headed for Des Moines. Louie didn't know how to drive but he kept the car on the road and made all the necessary stops. Two fifteen-year-olds alone in a car was great fun. We swore and smoked cigarettes and talked about driving. We drove around for an hour or two, and then returned the car to its spot. There were no beds in Louie's hut, just blankets.

Late in the morning we went into the house for breakfast. On the way, Louie grabbed an armload of scrap wood for the stove. He added some wood to an existing fire, and then washed out a bowl in cold water – they didn't have hot water. He mixed some pancake batter from scratch. We ate thick unleavened pancakes while his baby brother waddled around the cluttered little room with his wet diaper in the parenthesis of his bowed legs. His mother was still in bed and his brothers were outside. We kept quiet because his dad was sleeping.

Louie and I visited each other off and on for the rest of the summer. The highlight of each visit was stealing his dad's car. One night while we were cruising through Des Moines, the car suddenly quit running. We looked at each other. Louie tried to start it. It made weird noises.

"Now what?" I asked.

"We gotta go find help," Louie said.

We got out and hitchhiked off in search of help. I can't remember where we went or who helped us, but we got the car back in its spot before Louie's dad got home.

The next time I saw Louie I asked, "Did you find out why the car broke down?

"Timing gear broke. My dad fixed it. I watched him do it," he said.

"Did you get in trouble?"

"No. He doesn't know how it happened."

Across the street from Louie's house was an abandoned chicken farm. One of the fields was being developed into a new housing sub-division. A big sign invited buyers. "Thunder Bird Estates – Open house." Louie and I walked through the development checking out the houses. They were large California style ranch houses with ceiling to floor windows. The model home was furnished; even to include dishes and flowers – and cigarettes. As we walked through, we snuck cigarettes and put them in our pockets. We also noticed lumber scattered around. Being always on the lookout for building material, Louie said, "Let's come back tonight and get some of those boards."

That night we swiped Louie's dad's old Ford and headed for Des Moines. We drove through town on Marine View Drive and were about to turn at Des

Moines Memorial Drive, when Louie lost control in some gravel and slid into a guard post. It was around two in the morning. We stood looking at a huge dent. "I'm in trouble now", Louie said.

All I could say was, "Now what?"

The car looked terrible, but drivable. We got in and carefully drove the car back to its spot in front of Louie's place, but it now had only one head light.

"Louie," I said, "I can't stay. I'm afraid of your dad."

"Don't worry about it. He'll drive down to the house and never look at it," he said.

Reluctantly, I said. "Okay." and we crawled into Louie's hut.

Next morning after Louie fixed pancakes we stood and looked at the car.

"That's really bad," I observed.

The right front fender, bumper and headlight were pushed back just short of the front wheel.

"What are you going tell your dad?" I asked.

"Maybe we should roll it down the hill and leave it against a telephone pole. He'll think the brake failed." Louie suggested.

"Great idea," I said.

In the end Louie decided to tell the truth, or at least part of it. I went home.

A few days later I was back.

"What did your dad say?" I asked.

"Nothing. He knows about it but he didn't say anything."

"Are you going to tell him?"

"No."

"Guess what?" he added. "My brothers are in juvenile detention."

"What happened?"

Louie explained that his brothers sneaked into the model home at the Thunder Bird Estates. Everything would have been fine, except their dog followed them and got locked inside. The dog tore up the place looking for a way out. The next morning when the salesmen arrived, they let the dog out and watched it run home to the guilty brothers. They faced serious charges. I noticed a new pile of lumber in front of Louie's hut.

When school started, Louie and I didn't see much of each other. He started high school and I started my fourth year in junior high school. But I wisely avoided Federal Way and walked the mile to the nearest Highline bus stop. Over the summer, a new junior high school was finished, taking the load off of Puget Sound Junior High, where I went the year before. I enrolled in the new Sylvester Junior High School. It was on Sylvester Road near Bill Montgomery's house, Victor Colacurcio's place and Highline High School.

School was finally something to enjoy. In addition to regular classes I had woodshop, where I made a good looking bookshelf, and got a good grade doing it. I even participated in PE, and was selected for the boy's chorus. I had friends too.

In the first week of school I got caught with a fake cigarette. It was a paper tube with an orange tinfoil tip covered with a little ash and looked liked the real thing. I was in the auditorium standing on the stage showing it to some other kids when the coach saw it.

"Hey you, what's that in your hand?"

"Me?" I said.

"That's right. You."

He reached across the edge of the stage and grabbed my ankle. A quick pull and I was airborne, landing on the auditorium floor below the stage. He grabbed me by the neck and lifted me to my feet. He then propelled me into the principal's office. No principal ever saw a student on time, so I waited. Finally the principal stuck his head out. "Paul Strand?"

I got up and walked in.

"I hear you were smoking in the auditorium," he said.

"No Sir, I wasn't. It was a fake cigarette."

"But you wanted us to believe it was a real cigarette, didn't you?"

"I just wanted my friends to think it was real."

"Smoking in school is a serious infraction."

"I wasn't smoking."

"It's the same thing."

I gave up. "I'm sorry. I didn't mean to cause trouble. I'll never do anything like that again."

He threw the crumpled fake cigarette in his desk drawer, and accepted my apology. I left. The coach never mentioned the incident again and was actually nice to me. Some of the other students treated me like a celebrity.

Our low position in life moved up a notch when

When Grandpa Was a Kid

Mom moved us to a little log cabin behind the Blockhouse Restaurant where she worked. Both buildings were in the same log cabin style and were a brown hue. It was closer to my bus stop and inside the Highline School District. The only problem was I had to cross highway 99 to get there.

After school I often found a casserole waiting for me in the oven. If it wasn't there I made a bowl of instant pudding. Sometimes Mom let me go to the restaurant where she made a strawberry soda for me – my all time favorite treat.

The restaurant owner had a house on the same property and had a daughter my age who went to Highline High School (everyone my age went to high school, except me.) I sometimes watched TV with her after school. One evening she said she had a small surgery that temporarily made it difficult to sit. I teased her by bouncing around the floor on my bottom saying things like, "would that hurt?' Or, "Don't you wish you could do this?" Then I heard a snap and felt a sharp pain in the end of my spine. I had bent the little bones at end of my spine. Now I had a nagging pain that made it uncomfortable for *me* to sit -- served me right. Some years later I limped off of a tennis court and went to a chiropractor who popped it straight and I was instantly cured.

As Christmas approached, the school got ready for a Christmas concert. We practiced all the best Christmas carols and popular songs; the orchestra learned the music, the choir learned harmony and I sang base. I wasn't really a base, but most of the boys sounded like girls and they needed a lower complement. When Christmas came we performed first for the students and faculty during the day, then at night we gave a concert for parents. I was so nervous I twitched, but I had a wonderful time.

Before she left Richland, Mom met a cook where she worked. He followed her to Midway. His name was Willy Lee Wren, but everyone called him Bill. He was a tall skinny guy with a perpetual crooked smile like he knew something you didn't. His bright blue eyes always sparkled and his wavy blond hair was always neatly combed back. He was from Texas and had an accent that, while pleasant to hear, needed some interpretation. For example he called a mirror a "me row", get sounded like "git" and grease sounded like " greeze." He drove an old, but very new looking 1941 Hudson, bright blue with whitewall tires. He also liked to drink.

Bill had a seven-year-old son Duane, living with Bill's sister Adra, pronounced "Ader", who lived in Burlington, a little town sixty miles north of Seattle. Bill found work cooking at a truck stop in Mount Vernon, a town just three miles south of Burlington.

After Christmas Mom announced we were moving to Mount Vernon. For the first time in my life, I regretted leaving school, and was really tired of moving.

When Grandpa Was a Kid

Chapter 31

Mount Vernon

Mount Vernon was a small town next to a big river in a broad valley. It was the business hub for the surrounding territory, as well as the Skagit County seat. The Skagit River ran right through the middle, with high levies to keep it out of town and away from the farms. The Skagit Valley was mostly agricultural with nationally important seed crops, dozens of dairies, and millions of tulips. Wealthy people lived on a hill above town, everyone else lived in the valley below.

Mom and Bill went ahead to find a place to live. The night they arrived in town, Bill's car was stolen. The sheriff found it on a muddy little road in between some blackberry bushes. The car had been filled with our belongings. Mom searched the bushes for hours, retrieving family pictures and other valuables that were strewn around near the car. Much was missing including my stamp collection. Three Indian boys were convicted in the crime, but no missing property was recovered from them.

Our new home was in a large old house overlooking the valley on 4th Avenue. We rented three apartments on the lower floor. The owner lived in the two stories above us. The largest apartment had a view of the city, and was for Mom. Bill had his own apartment somewhere in the building, and I got an apartment all to myself. Most of the time, we all hung

When Grandpa Was a Kid

around Mom's apartment where we ate and watched TV.

Behind the house was a retaining wall that defined the edge of the new Interstate 5 freeway being constructed below us. The bulkhead between the freeway site and our place was back filled and muddy. Late one night, Mom heard a small dog barking and barking. It wouldn't stop. It didn't sound right, so Mom went to investigate. Not far from the house she saw a desperate little dog trying to pull a boy from the mud behind the bulkhead. He was up to his waist in mud and sinking. Mom went in after him. Thank God Mom was strong. She pulled him out and brought him home. She cleaned him up. Since we didn't have a phone, she took the boy upstairs to the landlady, who called the police. Next day the paper reported the close escape, but credited the landlady with the rescue. Mom was furious, since she had risked her own life and lost her new shoes saving the boy.

Paul age 15

A few blocks away was Lincoln Junior High School. It was old and sat on a residential street surrounded by nice homes and sidewalks. I enrolled in yet another school. Luckily, I was well received and given good classes including the school newspaper. Students were not used to new kids moving in. That

Mount Vernon

made me an oddity but I immediately attracted some friends.

The easiest friends to make are usually the outcasts. I met one who was a troublemaker. We went places together until one night when he mouthed off to a waitress as she cleaned a small café. We were the only two customers. I sat at the counter sipping a cherry coke and nibbling French fries. He got up and wandered around the café.

Tucked under the counter in front of me, stretched an eight foot long soda fountain. Soda fountains were popular for decades, but were almost all gone by 1955, thanks to fast foods and super markets. I leaned over for a closer look at the chrome and stainless steel marvel that held cartons of ice cream, and rows of sauce pumps and topping dippers. Two tall water and soda water dispensers arched above.

Behind me my soon to be ex-friend sneered at the waitress. "Trying to sweep the floor?" I heard him say, as he kicked a small pile of dust across the room.

I saw him in the mirror behind the counter between rows of ice cream dishes. The waitress stopped with her hands on her hips. She wasn't much older than us.

"How would you like to sweep that back up for me?" she said.

Then her head disappeared from my view behind a bunch of bananas hanging in front of the mirror ready for banana splits. I turned around for a more direct view.

"You do it," he said.

When Grandpa Was a Kid

"You better leave," she said.

"If I have to leave, I'm not paying."

"You boys leave now," she said. "I'm calling the police."

I put some money on the counter and grabbed a handful of fries. "Sorry," I said to the waitress, and walked out the door.

Police were a common sight in down town Mount Vernon. On Friday nights when the movies got out, police were posted in front of the theaters. The kids in town were either afraid of, or antagonistic toward Mexican crop works that also liked to go to the movies. Confrontations between the two groups were common. Some of the young Mexicans were dangerous and had proven so. They looked plenty scary to me with their slick black hair, tattooed hands and switchblade knives. As a result, all Mexicans were feared and parents demanded protection for their children.

A better friend was a kid named Egbert Museriue. Fortunately, people called him Buzz. He lived only a couple of blocks away in a rather large house. He said it had 23 rooms. I went home with him from school and was greeted by his very kind and pretty mother, who gave us snacks. We took our food downstairs to play pool. I ran into Buzz years later in the Army. It's a small world.

Another friend was Vernon Church. He lived just south of town in a little house next to the freeway construction. His house was also behind the Mount Vernon Church. Vern joked that it advertised where he lived.

Mount Vernon

In Vern's yard was a beat-up 1940 Ford sedan with a broken water pump. His stepdad let him take it out on the unfinished freeway. Construction had stopped, leaving a rough grade covered with tall grass and boulders. Sometimes, after school, Vern and I filled the radiator with cold water and took turns driving up and down the freeway on a dirt path we blazed, until the engine overheated. We were learning to drive. In the spring when construction resumed, the contractors used the trail we blazed.

Vern moved to a small farm in the woods south of the valley, but soon showed up driving a 1940 Chevrolet coupe. It was his, even though he was too young to drive. He took me and other friends all over the place in it, including the farm where he lived.

I could have had a car too. When I turned sixteen that April, Bill had a surprise for me.

"I found a car for you." He said. "It runs pretty good and only costs thirty-five dollars. We could fix it up pretty easy."

We went to have a look at it. I shrunk with embarrassment when I saw it. It was a 1935 dodge coupe, faded pea soup green with a small wooden pickup bed sticking out where the trunk lid had been. Grass was growing on it.

"What do you think?" he asked.

"I'm sorry, but I don't think so."

We left. That was the last such offer.

I continued to ride around with Vern. One rainy night on our way home from Burlington, a carload of American Indian boys fell in behind and began harassing us with their car. We sped up and they sped up. As we crossed the steel grating of the narrow bridge over the Skagit River, Their car slid sideways and spun around in the road until it plowed into the front row of cars in a new car dealership. We stopped and went back to see if they were okay. The Indian boys were getting out of the car. They looked okay, but one of them had blood on his face. We jumped back in the car and got out of there. I wondered if they had anything to do with my stolen stamp collection. The next day the newspaper said they were forced off the road by a carload of boys.

The Skagit River drained a good part of northwestern Washington and a small part of British Columbia. It had several tributaries. When it rained, the river rose. Flooding was common. This year it flooded more than usual. From our window we could see the water spread beyond the river to the west of town. Later when the water subsided, Buzz and I went to a slough across from town where boats had collected. The good ones had been retrieved but we found a small rowboat. We made paddles from pieces of boards and ventured into the slough. We paddled to the end of it and looked at the mighty waters of the Skagit River racing by. We turned back for shore and forgot about boating on the river.

Every spring, in Mount Vernon, some high school students began initiating certain eighth graders into high school. Targets for hazing were students who stood out in some way. It started on a sunny Saturday afternoon in May. Buzz, Vern and I were walking along Main Street when a car load of boys went past yelling insults at us.

"You guys think you're pretty smart. Don't you?"

Another one yelled, "Better keep your eyes open. We're going to kick the crap out of ya!"

We knew we were in trouble. Buzz told us what to expect.

"They're going to kidnap us and beat us up," he said.

He went on to tell the fate of others before us.

"One kid was taken out in the woods and tied naked to a tree and left there overnight," he said.

"What happened to him?" Vern asked.

"The Sheriff found him. He was covered with honey, left for the bears to eat."

Then he told us about a killing.

"They took somebody out to a lake, and went out to the end of a dock were they pulled his pants down and made him grab his ankles. Then they hit him with a board and knocked him into the lake and he drowned."

I believed him. Buzz seemed sincere and truly afraid of initiation. Then he pointed up to a hotel window just down the street.

"They hung a guy out the window by his heels and threatened to drop him."

"How do you know?" Vern asked.

"Everybody knows," he said. "Stuff like that happens every year."

We turned onto a side street and continued our conversation. Just then a carload of high school boys pulled up. A car door opened and we took off running. Buzz and Vern were ahead of me and turned into an ally, running full speed. I turned into the ally right behind them, and ducked behind some garbage cans. The high school boys ran right past and out the other end of the ally, bent on catching my friends. I got up and ran the other way.

On Sunday afternoon, Vern knocked on the door. "What happened to you?"

"Nothing," I said, "I hid from them. Did they catch you?"

"No. We ran into a store," Vern said.

Then I posed a question. "Do those guys only want us and not Buzz.?

Vern summed up what I was thinking. "Buzz is from a well-known family. I don't think they'd hurt him," he said.

"Then it's you and me."

"Not me," Vern said.

He was right. He never did anything that attracted attention to himself. They didn't even know who he was.

The next Saturday they caught me. Their car pulled up beside me on Montgomery Street. I was immediately surrounded and pulled into the car. I had been kidnapped.

They took me to a clearing in some woods on a hill east of town. We all got out. My worst fears were coming true. Just like Buzz's story.

"You ready to fight?" one asked me.

There were four of them. I said, "No."

Mount Vernon

"What's the matter? Are you a chicken?"

"No"

"Go ahead, you hit first."

"I don't want to fight."

"Chicken shit," he said. The biggest guy did all the talking. "Do you think you could beat me up?" he said.

"No."

He pointed his finger at the littlest guy and asked, "Do think you could beat him up?"

I sized up the skinny runt, who turned pale with fright. "No." I said.

"Let's tie him up." The big guy said.

It was just like Buzz said. They were going to leave me here for the bears to eat. I always carried a pocketknife. I slipped my hands casually into my pockets. One hand firmly gripped my knife. I would not be tied naked to a tree. I was terrified and stopped talking. I stood quietly with my hands in my pockets while my tormentors continued with threats and taunts. I was acting so casual that they weren't having any more fun. They eventually got back in the car and left. I spent the rest of the afternoon walking back to town.

In June I graduated from the eighth grade, without any further initiation. Four years of high school to go. I had no plans at all of graduating from high school at age twenty. But for now I had a summer ahead of me. Right away, Mom asked me if I wanted to stay with Mavis for a while. "Sure." I said. She gave me a little money and put me on a bus.

When Grandpa Was a Kid

Chapter 32

The Last Summer of Childhood

After I got settled in at Mavis' house I hitchhiked around to do some visiting. Vern Church who left Mount Vernon when I did, was living in South Seattle. Also, a girl from our class moved to Kent. I visited them, but it wasn't the same so I didn't go back.

I also visited my Grandma and Grandpa Landgren in our old house in Midway. Mom's chalk art work was still on the wall and the same furniture was still in the same places. Grandma opened our old Frigidaire and offered me some lunch. The thing was almost empty. A bowl with two little boiled potatoes and one chicken leg sat in the middle of the shelf. Grandma heated them up and served me lunch. I was hungry so it actually tasted good. I had no idea what to talk about, so after answering a few questions about Mom I left.

Mavis was living in a wooded area east of Renton. I noticed right away that her piano was missing. She said they had to leave her piano at the rented farmhouse because Ernie couldn't pay the rent. He was also out of work again. Neither Ernie nor I had anything to do, so we rode around together in whatever his current old beat up toilet of a car was. Ernie always had a car, but on his budget they didn't last long and were the cheapest contraptions money could buy.

Ernie decided to go to the Seattle Public Market to

pick up some groceries, and took me along. The narrow Pike Place was crowded with delivery trucks and shoppers. But it was a weekday and we found a spot in front of some unused stalls. We walked past some empty stalls to a meat market. Ernie bought horse meat.

"I thought you weren't supposed to eat horse meat," I said.

"It's good," he said.

"What else are you going to get, dog meat?" I asked.

"You'll like it. You just have to be careful not to cook the sweat glands."

On a hallway behind the horse meat vendor's table was a donut shop with a view of Elliott Bay and the new Alaska Way Viaduct. We sat and drank a bottle of Coke. Ernie never drank coffee. Out on the bay a ferryboat was coming in from Bremerton. It was stream lined with a row of little round windows down the side.

I pointed it out to Ernie and said, "That's the Kalakala. Mom used to work on it."

When we finished we went downstairs to a mostly abandoned hallway. At one end was a specialties store. They sold unusual foods from around the world. Ernie bought a tiny can of caviar. We exited the Market by a side door that opened to a set of wooden stairs that ran from Western Avenue, well below the cliff that the Pike Place Market was built on, and up to the main level on Pike Street. We went up to Pike Street and back to the car.

The Last Summer of Childhood

At home Ernie cooked the meat like steaks. It was very lean, but tasted good. I passed on the caviar.

Another trip was to Ernie's parent's place. I liked Zola and was anxious to visit. We were out in the back yard when Ernie said, "I'll be right back." He went in the house and came out with a .22-caliber rifle. He aimed it at me and fired. Whack! I was hit in the leg. It stung, but the bullet fell to the ground. Ernie started laughing and I started swearing. He had emptied the powder from a cartridge. The bullet was propelled only by the energy of the firing cap. It only had enough power to sting, not penetrate. I sounded just like my dad when I waved my finger at Ernie, and said, "What's the matter with you? Don't you know better than to pull a stunt like that?"

Ernie laughed at his juvenile joke, but I remained stern until he finally said, "Sorry." I was tired of his juvenile behavior and his inability to support his family.

While Ernie and I were fooling around doing nothing, Mom and Bill were in California getting married. We found out about it after the fact, when Mom and Bill showed up in an almost new, yellow, 1953 Packard Clipper. They looked like two movie stars home from Hollywood. Actually they had been in San Jose.

Mom said that we were going to have a new home, but not anything like Hollywood. Bill proudly announced that he was the new manager of a restaurant in Moses Lake.

"Where's Moses Lake?" I asked.

"It's over in the Columbia Basin," Bill said.
"It's where?"
"Eastern Washington."

The plans were already made. Mom would stay in Mount Vernon while Bill and I went to Moses Lake to find a house. Then Mom and Bill's son Duane would follow.

Eastern Washington was hot. We rode with the windows down as the sleek Packard glided along the highway through the brown desert. Heat waves rose from the pavement and made the road ahead of us look like shimmering pools of cool blue water. Then we saw some real water in the distance. Wide and blue, Moses Lake was one of the largest lakes in the state. It spread out like a still river that ran beside us as we approached the distant town.

That night, we stayed in a small, borrowed trailer house in Moses Lake. The mosquitoes ate us alive. One flew into my ear and got stuck. I flipped off the couch and squirmed around on the floor beating my head with my fist until the blood sucking monster was out of my ear. I finally got back to sleep listening to the whine of mosquitoes from where I hid under my blanket.

Bill spent half the next morning haggling over trailer houses. We started out looking at one with three tiny bedrooms. As the morning wore on they kept getting smaller until we finally wound up with one that had only one small bedroom.

It turned out to be my fault that we got such a

The Last Summer of Childhood

small place to live. Bill had borrowed the down payment from my grandpa. As I sat and listened to Bill and the dealer argue about not enough down payment, I said the obvious. "Why don't you just borrow some more money from Grandpa?"

That wrecked the whole deal. Apparently borrowed down payments were supposed to be a secret. Now the mortgage loan was denied and Bill had to settle for a cheaper trailer house. I didn't get yelled at until the deal was over and we were back in the car.

"When grownups talk business you should keep your mouth shut." Bill scolded. He was really angry.

I kept my next comment to myself, *Why didn't you go to a different dealer?*

The dealer parked our new home on a little space next to Bill's boss' trailer in the little community of Black's Addition on the edge of town. Mom and Duane arrived a few days later.

I happily ran into an old friend from the Airline Trailer Park in Bow Lake, Rodney Forester. He had arrived in Moses Lake the year before. He only lived about three dirt roads away. Like me he moved around too much and was also a sixteen-year-old ninth grader. I learned that most of the kids in Moses Lake were new, and that several of them were behind in school. A bunch more kids came to Moses Lake with the Air Force. I fit right in.

Rodney showed me around town and took me places he thought I'd like. Moses Lake had one main street which was also US Highway 10 and another street, Third Avenue, which was mostly under construction with new buildings being added.

It seemed like it never cooled off, great weather for wandering around town in the late evening. There were two theaters that changed their movies twice a week. The Lake Theater was new and clean. We went to that one. The other theater was smaller and old. Once a week it played Spanish language movies. Early movies got out while it was still daylight enough to wander around town some more.

A favorite hangout for kids was Shad's fountain. It stayed open late with young people hanging around inside and standing around outside. One night on a warm sidewalk in front of Shad's Fountain, Rodney introduced me to a girl he knew. She was beautiful. She aroused feelings in me that let me know that I was no longer a boy.

That wasn't the only event that marked the passing of my childhood. I no longer had thoughts of bicycles, electric trains or comic books. I gave them away. I thought of money and cars, new clothes and rock and roll music, and a lot about the future. Life was different here in Moses Lake and so was I. I was excited by all that lay ahead. I had new friends, new clothes, money in my pocket, and a full-time job washing dishes grave-yard shift in the hot kitchen of Nona's Café.

Epilogue

At age sixteen I was a young adult ready for the vast future that I so much looked forward to, but I had to wait for my mental and emotional maturity to catch up.

I quit school at 17 and went to stay with my dad, who was back in the greenhouse business at the Bow Lake farm. After my eighteenth birthday I worked for the Boeing Airplane Company as a riveter, and then finished most of an apprentice carpenter program. During my apprenticeship I enlisted in the Army, after which I enrolled in college.

Although I spent my school years looking out of the window of more than 20 schools, I attended Eastern Washington University, graduating in the top third of my class. I then worked 30 years for the State of Washington as a caseworker, research analyst, computer programmer and finally an information systems supervisor. After that, I operated a home based web design business for several years.

At the time of this writing I am retired and living in Lacey, Washington with my wife Karen of twenty years. We are a blended family with several children and 23 grandchildren between us. It is with them in mind that I wrote this memoir.

To order this book
or for more information
about this book or its author
contact Paul Strand at
pstrand2000@comcast.net

Made in the USA
Charleston, SC
20 February 2012